Subrata Dasgupta is Dire... Science and holder of the ... Computer Science at the Un... is the author of nine prev... fiction *Three Times a M*... He lives in Louisiana.

Also by Subrata Dasgupta

Creativity in Invention and Design
(Cambridge University Press, 1994).

Technology and Creativity (Oxford University Press, 1996).

Jagadis Chandra Bose and the Indian Response to Western Science
(Oxford University Press, 1999).

Three Times a Minority (Writers Workshop, 2003).

*Twilight of the Bengal Renaissance: R. K. Dasgupta and His Quest
for a World Mind* (Dey's Publishing, 2005).

SALAAM
Stanley Matthews

SUBRATA DASGUPTA

Granta Books
London

Granta Publications, 2/3 Hanover Yard, London N1 8BE

First published in Great Britain by Granta Books 2006

Copyright © 2006 by Subrata Dasgupta

Subrata Dasgupta has asserted his moral right under the
Copyright, Designs and Patents Act, 1988, to be
identified as the author of this work.

A CIP catalogue record for this book
is available from the British Library.

1 3 5 7 9 10 8 6 4 2

ISBN-13: 978 1 86207 812 3
ISBN-10: 1 86207 812 2

Typeset by M Rules
Printed and bound in Italy
by Legoprint

To

'Mimi': Manju Gupta

&

'Mamu': Milan Chandra Gupta

and their daughters

Bishnupriya & Monobina

Acknowledgements

This book has a long history, evolving through several incarnations. I am indebted to my agent Anne Dewe for keeping faith with the work. I also thank Burton Raffel, Tirthankar Bose and Mithu Dasgupta – the first readers of an early version of this story. My son Shome Dasgupta read the work with a young man's eye and assured me that the world of my boyhood is not so alien to someone of his generation. An anonymous reader offered advice that I took seriously and gratefully. Finally, I thank my editor Fatema Ahmed: it has been a pleasure working with her.

Contents

Prelude

Thursday 24 February 2000. **Sir Stanley Matthews is dead.** *The man who in his time was the most famous footballer in the world, the sport's first knight, who graced the game for thirty years and played his last one a few days after his fiftieth birthday, passed away peacefully yesterday at the age of eighty-five in a hospital near his birthplace, Stoke-on-Trent.*

At the match at Wembley between England and Argentina, both teams wore black armbands and, along with several thousand spectators, bowed their heads in tribute to the Maestro.

Last night, on television chat shows, on the radio, on websites, and in statements to the press, people who had known Sir Stanley personally, players who had played with and against him, and journalists who had once written about him, reflected on the man. They remembered his greatest games. They recalled the magic and the mystery of his art, his bursts of speed, his swerve, the 'dummies' he 'sold' to countless, hapless left backs, his loping, bandy-legged run, his pinpoint-accurate pass from almost the goal line, his obsessive fitness, his spartan habits, his modesty and diffidence, his sportsmanship, his obdurate disinclination to score goals. Several television channels reran highlights from the Matthews Cup Final. *They showed scratchy, jerky newsreel footage of his international triumphs spanning a quarter of a century, from his brilliant performance in the infamous match against Germany in 1938 – watched by Goering, Goebbels and Ribbentrop, when the England team were pressured into giving the Nazi salute – to his mastery of the Brazilian side in 1956, when he was all of forty-two.*

Across Great Britain, on the Continent, in South America, and whenever football and its history are revered, men (and many women) whose once young lives were touched and illuminated by his magic, will mourn the passing of Sir Stanley Matthews.

I composed this obituary after hearing the news in an email from a cousin in Kolkata. But, somehow, it failed to capture what I felt, and I realized that no conventional obituary of Stanley Matthews, no biography, not even his autobiography could explain how important he was to me. He was not just a footballing hero; to me he represents a large slice of my memories: my life as a Bengali boy who grew up in 1950s England. Remembering Stanley Matthews is how I remember this boyhood.

SALAAM
Stanley Matthews

1

The Number Eleven

In 1950, when I was six years old, I boarded the S.S. *Jal Jawahar* in Bombay (now Mumbai) with my mother and grandmother. Our destination was England, or *Bilat* as it is called in colloquial Bengali. The sea voyage took about three weeks and it was a completely new experience for me. There were many British people on board and it was the first time I had seen so many of them in one place. Their presence prompted me to acquire my first phrases of English by the time the voyage was over. If nothing else, I learned English politeness; to the great amusement of my mother and grandmother I would say 'thank you' and 'excuse me' at every opportunity, whether appropriate or not.

We docked at Liverpool one gloomy, foggy morning, but the weather did nothing to diminish my excitement at seeing my father for the first time in fifteen months. He had spent a year studying in Rome for postgraduate qualifications in his speciality (ear, nose and throat) before moving to London a few months before we arrived.

Just after he reached London, my father wrote me a letter describing the city. He admired its streets – not a scrap of paper or rubbish anywhere on the streets and pavements, he said. There were things called zebra crossings, white stripes across the street guarded by poles with blinking orange balls on top called Belisha beacons (he drew a picture of these), and when someone wanted to cross the street at these places, cars would come to a standstill. He wrote that in London trains ran deep below the ground, and that people went down to catch these trains, called tubes, on moving staircases known as escalators. And because he was a gifted artist, he also sent me a meticulous ink drawing of an escalator, complete with an illustration of its inner mechanism. My cousins and I in Calcutta (now Kolkata) marvelled at this drawing for days afterwards.

My first and most vivid impression of London was of how cold and damp and grey it was and of the plumes of smoke rising from countless chimneys. My father had his own living quarters in the hospital where he was working as a registrar, so he got us a tiny flat within walking distance of the hospital, at number 23 Warwick Road, not far from Earls Court tube station. It was at this tube station, only days after our arrival, that I saw my first escalator, a sight that filled me with awe and my grandmother with fear at the prospect of stepping onto it. Near the Earls Court Exhibition Centre, I stood quite still and took a deep breath of exhilaration on spotting my first Belisha beacon.

On weekdays my father lived in his hospital rooms and came to us in the evening for dinner. On weekends he would come home and stay with us at Warwick Road. Our flat was opposite a school called St Matthias and this was where I began my English education. My class teacher had once lived in India and knew some Hindi, which was an immense relief, for although I had learned a little English on the ship I was still uncertain of myself and, at least, I had a smattering of Hindi. I was afraid that if my teacher and the other children thought I could speak

English they might ask me questions or say things I would not understand at all, and so make me feel and look foolish. As a precaution, for the first few weeks I spoke almost no English at all, happy to communicate with the teacher in pidgin Hindi. Yet, I must have become comfortable in English quite quickly, for at the class Christmas party I was able to join in with the others and sing various party songs with great gusto – including, I recall, a song called 'Ten green bottles hanging on the wall'. The inanity of the words struck me even then, but at least I understood them.

Number 23 Warwick Road was far from satisfactory, but it was the most convenient place my father could find for us at short notice. Our flat was on the top floor and consisted of two rooms: one large room which served simultaneously as a bedsitter, a kitchenette and a dining room, and a tiny adjoining room where my grandmother and I slept. In the larger room there was a sink and a two-ring gas stove on a table on one side, a sofa on the other, and a double bed in the centre. The toilet was a floor and a half below, and the bathroom somewhere else – I can no longer recall. What I do remember vividly is the misery of waking up in the middle of those cold winter nights and, needing to pee, I would stumble, shivering, down the steep, creaking stairs which were barely covered by a threadbare carpet.

It was a warren of a house. There were at least five other families, mostly young couples, some with babies. You could hear the babies crying all day long. The landlord and his wife, Mr and Mrs Wilson, lived in the basement. Perhaps my father had rented this flat because the Wilsons were Anglo-Indians. Perhaps he thought we would feel more comfortable with them because they were originally from Calcutta.

Mrs Wilson was slim and pretty in a garish sort of way. She always wore long, colourful earrings, scarlet lipstick, and slacks –

to my mother's and grandmother's Bengali eyes, this last detail relegated Mrs Wilson to a particular social stratum. 'Nice' women – even nice *English* women – they believed, did not wear trousers. As for me, I had never seen women in slacks, not even on board the S.S. *Jal Jawahar*. I would stare at Mrs Wilson in silent fascination.

I was also puzzled by their English surname. How could they be Indian? I wondered. They were *Anglo*-Indians, my parents said: the descendants of British men who had once lived in India and married Indian women.

I was soon quite at ease in this house of strangers. In Calcutta I had been brought up in a large joint family and was used to being surrounded by people. I made friends with some of our co-tenants, and very soon I was spending a great deal of my spare time with one or the other of the families on the floors below, playing snakes and ladders or ludo or simple card games. As for my mother, she, too, found a niche for herself in the house. Peering down from the balcony on the top floor I would often see her sitting on the staircase near the ground floor with a few of the other women tenants. Despite my grandmother's presence, my mother was already beginning to miss the boisterous social life of our home in Calcutta: the laughter, the musical events, the amateur theatricals. She especially missed her brother and sister, the cousins and nephews and nieces, who had been integral to her life both in her parents' home and in that of her in-laws. Her new friends helped to distract her a little from the beginnings of a homesickness that never entirely went away over the next eight years.

London itself did not help. The war had ended five years earlier but its after-effects were visible everywhere. Even I, blissfully ignorant of what had actually taken place, could sense something was amiss, a kind of deprivation in this new world around me.

Some food items were still rationed; buildings blackened at the time of the Blitz were still black; and then there were the street musicians – buskers of sorts – with black patches to hide unseeing eyes, or without arms or legs. They had fought in the war, my father explained. Even the Festival of Britain in 1951, which we attended several times, seemed, to my eyes, full of desperate and forced jollity. I didn't find it very festive.

About six months after our arrival in London, my father moved out of his hospital quarters and we all shifted to another, more comfortable and completely self-contained, flat on Cromwell Road. Its distinctive features were a chandelier in the living room, our own bathroom and toilet; and the fact that I had a tiny room of my own. The flat was still near enough St Matthias's that I could walk to school escorted by my mother and sometimes, if it was not too cold, my grandmother. Unfortunately, we were to enjoy this relatively luxurious flat for only six months. My father took a position at the Nottingham General Hospital, and moved there ahead of us, visiting us in London at weekends until, some time in January 1952, we too moved to Nottingham: to 22 Cavendish Crescent.

In later years, Nottingham would become firmly associated in my mind with its football clubs. But in the two years we there, I knew nothing of Nottingham Forest or Nottingham County. For me, Nottingham, and Trent Bridge in particular, was where they played cricket, not football – and test cricket at that. I date the beginning of my English boyhood to the summer of 1952. It all began with cricket.

In March, my mother, grandmother and I returned to Calcutta to attend my uncle's wedding. After the festivities, my grandmother remained in India and my mother and I returned to England on a plane which was also carrying the Indian cricket team. The seats were arranged so that two passengers sat

My grandmother, uncle, parents and me in London in 1950.

opposite another pair of passengers. My mother and I sat across from the Indian test captain, Vijay Hazare.

The Indian wicketkeeper, Probir Sen, was one of only two Bengalis in the Indian side at that time and his family were friends of my mother's family, as was the Indian team manager. And so, when India came to play England in the Trent Bridge test match I went along to watch with my mother. I must have boasted at school that I knew some of the players, for the principal, a tall nun who always carried a leather strap in her hand, persuaded my parents to have a book about cricket autographed by both the Indian and English teams as a gift for some lucky pupil at prizegiving.

My mother agreed to the principal's request and I accompanied her into the pavilion at Trent Bridge to collect the autographed book. I no longer remember if I managed to get some autographs for myself, though.

Nottingham held other, more compelling, mysteries for a child of seven. It was, after all, Robin Hood country. I may not have known Nottingham Forest, the football club, but I knew of Nottingham Forest. I don't think that we ever actually went into the forest although I saw it from a distance. But this didn't matter, because much nearer to where we lived, within walking distance, stood Nottingham Castle, and whenever family friends visited us from London or Lincoln or Stafford or Derby or an aunt or uncle came from Calcutta, we would take them to the castle and show them the bronze statue of Robin Hood. To be honest, I never liked the statue, for it had no resemblance *at all* to my mental picture of the great man, which was, essentially, the image of Errol Flynn in the Robin Hood movie.

Then there was the Goose Fair every October. Many years later, reading J. B. Priestley's *English Journey*, I learned that this went back to the Middle Ages. Much to my embarrassment I once vomited at the fair, after going on one of those rides – the awful kind in which one is whirled round and round and up and down in one, continuous, stomach-churning motion. My father loved trying the games on the stalls and would win one prize after another, worthless trinkets for the most part except for one memorable time when, to my mother's delight, he won a fine tablecloth made of Nottingham lace.

My school, St Joseph's, had a large playground but no playing fields. To play cricket that summer, we were bussed to green fields belonging to Nottingham University. I was overjoyed at the thrill of donning real pads, real batting gloves, even wearing abdominal guards – though they rubbed horribly against my inner thighs when I ran between wickets. And the thrill of wielding real bats with Len Hutton's signature on them, and of wearing white cable-stitch sweaters with V-necks – just like the test players! The pleasure lay almost entirely in the play-acting, for I realized that real playing was a different experience altogether. Standing at the crease watching a fast-bowling schoolmate come tearing down at me, I felt a terror I never knew existed. Was this what Vinoo Mankad felt, I wondered, when he faced Freddie Truman? Did he have the same impulse to flee? But then, once in a while, I would feel a thrill as great as my former terror, when by some miracle of timing and hand–eye coordination and footwork, I would make proper contact with the ball, right in the centre of the bat, the way our cricket master told us it should be done. The hard, red, leather ball which a moment earlier had been hurtling menacingly towards me, in that instant, obeyed my command. It went where I wanted, where I desperately hoped it would go.

English summers are all too short, unlike the Indian summers I still remembered from when we lived in Calcutta. Summer in Calcutta begins around the time of the Bengali New Year, the first day of the Bengali month of *Baisakh*, in mid-April – though sometimes it would start even earlier, interrupting spring. And though the monsoon rains would give some relief from the heat, summer in Calcutta did not really end until October, at about the time when the *Durga Puja*, Bengal's main religious event, was celebrated, and there was in the air not only the noise, bustle and the colour of the festivities, but a mellowing of the sun's heat, the wistful promise of winter which was Calcutta's most desired season. My birthday, 18 October, usually fell on one or another of the four *Puja* days. One of my last birthdays in India, my fourth or fifth, was on the day of *ashtami*, the second and most auspicious day of the festivities. One of my oldest cousins had set up a loudspeaker outside the house that we all shared, the whole joint family of parents, uncles, aunts, siblings and cousins, and I woke early on the day of *ashtami* to the sound of a song booming out of the speaker. Perhaps it was a *Durga Puja* song, or perhaps it was one of my mother's many recordings of *Rabindra-sangeet*, the songs of Rabindranath Tagore. Whatever it was, the fact that it was played for me and the fact that this most auspicious *Durga Puja* day was my birthday, made me dizzy with happiness and self-importance. I went round touching my elders' feet, an act called *pronum* in Bengali, and they in turn gave me their blessings, placing their palms down on my head.

There was no festival of Durga in Nottingham, however, and the summer had ended long before October. Instead of the six-foot-tall clay statue of Durga and her entourage which was erected every year in the lane outside our house in north Calcutta (it was brought by lorry from the image-maker's shanty hut in a remote suburb and placed in the *pandal*, a kind of tent made of bamboo poles and covered with red and white and blue cloth), here at 22 Cavendish Crescent we had to make do with an eight-by-five-inch colour photo of Durga. Instead of a congregation of fifty or sixty relatives, and scores of neighbours and friends, we had to be content – and my parents were grateful, I think – to have with us just a few homesick Bengali bachelors. Their fathers had shipped them abroad to learn practical engineering at English firms scattered around the Midlands.

These bachelors, mostly in their early twenties – I called them all 'this-*da*' or 'that-*da*' (*da*, a diminutive of *dada* in Bengali, meaning an older brother or male cousin or in lieu thereof) – loved to visit us, one of the few Bengali families in the Midlands. At weekends or on occasions like the *Durga Puja* they stole away from their bleak, lonely lives in digs and hopeless English food prepared by their landladies, some well-meaning, some indifferent, some downright ill-tempered who hated their lodgers to use the toilet late at night because the noise of the flush would disturb them. They converged on Nottingham from all over the Midlands and the Potteries to partake of special *Puja* food cooked by my mother, whom they addressed as Protima-*di* (*di*, a diminutive of *didi* in Bengali, meaning an older sister or female cousin) – for she was the collective surrogate for all their older sisters back home.

My mother would have cooked a proper Bengali meal for them. She would have made *daal*, perhaps a vegetable dish to accompany it – squash or cauliflower or aubergine – and a rich mutton curry to follow. And after they had eaten, and the plates and dishes had been washed and dried, they would light cigarettes and ask my mother to sing. She would oblige with a song by Tagore, and then another, and yet another, then perhaps a popular Hindi film song. As the afternoon merged into early evening and time for dinner, they played Monopoly or ludo, and told each other stories of the girls they had met in shoddy dance halls – most of whom, the bachelors would candidly and ruefully admit, rebuffed them because (it was their unanimous view) they were not white.

To me, these Bengali bachelors seemed quite old but they

were young men, in their early twenties for the most part. Their families were affluent enough to send their sons abroad although, given the choice, they would have preferred them to go to British universities – Glasgow or Manchester or Leeds or London – to study engineering and return with prestigious degrees. Some of them would have been unable to afford this, while others might not have been good enough to get into a British university. So the next best thing was to be apprenticed to the great British engineering firms which had almost mythical reputations in India: Rolls-Royce, International Combustion, Larsen & Toubro, Simon Carves. And as I had no brothers and sisters of my own, and my cousins were thousands of miles away, these Bengali bachelors became my elder brothers, my *dadas*.

When the summer ended so did cricket. The Indian team had lost the test series, and twice made the wrong kind of history; once at Headingley where in the second innings they lost the first four wickets before a single run was scored, and again at Old Trafford where they were bowled out twice in the same day (Freddie Truman took eight wickets for thirty-one runs in eight furious overs). I could only accept my classmates' taunting in silence (I had nothing to say) and by the end of summer I had shed the last vestiges of my loyalty to Indian cricket: I became a fan of the English cricket team.

In school, cricket gave way to football. As in the summer, we were shepherded to the playing fields near the university, except now these same fields, that had felt so kindly and freshly-mown-pleasant-smelling then, looked menacing in the mist-enveloped autumn afternoons which were already threatening to give way to winter.

My first experience with the game did not impress me much. All that seemed to happen, as far as I could tell, was that a huge number of us rushed in collective pursuit of the ball as it bounced

A few homesick Bengali bachelors.

around the field. I obediently followed my classmates chasing the ball but did so with little conviction; I missed the measured, harmonious order of the summer game.

However, in those first days on the football field, I was completely fascinated by the goalkeepers standing tall and serious, in splendid isolation, between their goalposts. Sometimes I couldn't even see them, especially if the play was at one end of the field; the goalie at the other end would be swallowed up entirely in the mist and gloom. And then, when the ball strayed into the other half and we tore after it, he would magically reappear. The goalkeepers seemed like guardians of some sacred, unspoken trust as they bore the heavy responsibility of being the last line of defence. To add to their mystique, their apartness, they did not even dress like the rest of us: they did not wear the same shirts we wore but bright orange or yellow polo-neck jerseys. My lifelong fondness for polo-neck sweaters was born on the cold, muddy playing fields of Nottingham University. I desperately wanted one for myself and asked my mother to knit a bright red one for my approaching birthday.

That birthday was my eighth, and my parents threw a grand party for me. This was the first time I had celebrated my birthday in the Western sense, with cakes, candles and guests singing 'Happy Birthday'. My mother basked in the opportunity it gave her to entertain in style, in the manner she had acquired and cultivated in her own luxurious parental home.

I invited several of my classmates and such was the appeal of my party (there was an element of the exotic in being invited to an Indian's home), at least one boy *asked* to be invited. It was arranged that my mother and I would meet my classmates near one of the big stone lions in front of the City Hall in Market Square. We then escorted them to our house by bus. My best friend Christopher Floyd came and there was the girl with whom

I danced most often in the weekly singing and dancing class; I had kissed her at another girl's birthday party a few weeks earlier. We played party games, not the usual ones like musical chairs but one or two that my mother had dredged up from recollections of her own girlhood and others from a book she had bought called *One Hundred Party Games*.

We invited all the other inhabitants of 22 Cavendish Square, of course. They formed a rich, multinational menagerie: Mr and Mrs Todd, who owned the house; the Scottish army captain with a beautiful wife whose breath smelt permanently of whisky; a Canadian couple; an American couple who took pictures of my birthday party with their very expensive camera – their accents fascinated me, made my mother laugh, and were mimicked accurately, but affectionately and in private by my father. Then there were the Thomases. Mrs Thomas became my particular friend in the house. She was not beautiful in the way the Scottish captain's alcoholic wife was, nor even as pretty as the Canadian lady, but she entranced me the very first day we met – perhaps because of her hair which, I told her, was the colour of burnt sienna. Amused, she wanted to know how I knew. I showed her a bottle labelled Burnt Sienna from my box of poster paints. The colour matched her hair.

Mrs Thomas did not work – few married women did then – and I often visited her after school. The Thomases occupied a large bedsitter next to our two-room flat, and what most held my attention was a large, framed picture on their wall. It showed a snowy, winter scene in the foreground, and houses, and what looked like factories in the background. The picture teemed with colour and people and movement. It was a print, Mrs Thomas told me, of a painting by an English artist named L. S. Lowry.

The picture made a strong impression on me, for an unusual reason. For despite my initially unfavourable impressions of football, my imagination had been captured slowly by this winter game: its colour, motion, sound, the smell of the chilly air in which it was played whenever we went for our weekly games. The vibrancy of Lowry's painting – the contrast it made with the Thomases' drab bedsitter – reinforced my creeping fascination with football. And when I learned that Mrs Thomas was an amateur artist, and she learned that I liked to paint, we came up with the idea that we might do a painting together, a picture in the Lowry style. It would show a village with houses and streets and one or two shops, a church and perhaps a school and a hospital. There would be people walking about, sitting on benches, going to the church, running about or standing in small groups. There would be dogs and cats, of course. And in the middle of all this there would be a football game in progress – with goalies wearing polo-neck sweaters . . .

Soon after, Mrs Thomas bought a huge sheet of paper, and pinned it to an easel. Every afternoon, when I returned home from school, I gulped down my tea and rushed next door where the painting-in-progress stood in repose. Each day (and also at weekends), Mrs Thomas and I worked together steadily for an hour or two, adding a figure here, an object there. On weekdays, we would paint away until Mr Thomas came home. On some evenings our camaraderie was so complete, we were so utterly wrapped up in what we were doing that I resented Mr Thomas's re-entry into our orbit. The spell would be broken and I would wish that Mr Thomas worked late like my father. Mrs Thomas would put down her brush, wipe her fingers on her paint-smeared smock, and make a wry face to me – the session was over for that day, her face said. She would go over to her husband, they would kiss and then walk arm-in-arm out to their miniscule kitchen. Sometimes I would be asked to join them for a slice of cake or apple pie.

My obsession with the painting was total. I had no time nor inclination to visit the Todds' flat after dinner to watch cowboy films on television as I had done before – not even *Hopalong Cassidy*, my favourite, could entice me. I was spellbound by the project before us, and by my first experience of the creative act. I watched with amazement as the 'canvas' began to fill. The vision before us changed kaleidoscopically almost every evening. The picture took on a whimsical life of its own. Sometimes, a bare tree, a house, or the figure of a person which we added one evening – when it had looked so perfect that Mrs Thomas and I would congratulate each other before packing up for the night – looked utterly wrong the next day and we removed it.

For me, every detail was a preliminary to the real focus of the painting: the football game. Everything else was backdrop. When the rest was finished, I assumed command of the football scene. Mrs Thomas interjected only to correct something that did not look quite right. Once, early on, she pointed out that the size of the football field I had outlined was perhaps too large in proportion to the other objects in the painting. But the most important objection she raised was that there were too many players on the field. It was then that I realized, to my great embarrassment, that I didn't know that a football team had only eleven players! I had never actually bothered to count the players on my side when we went on our weekly trips to the playing fields. Even as I felt stupid about my ignorance, I was struck by the coincidence that both cricket and football had the same number of players in a team. I wondered why, but no one I asked could tell me. I still don't know the answer.

Finally, the painting was done. Gazing at the myriad people, animals, trees and houses strewn across the huge sheet of paper – the 'canvas' – I could hardly believe that this sheet had once been entirely blank. Mrs Thomas and I looked at each other and smiled.

The painting stayed on the easel for several weeks. The other occupants of our little community viewed it with admiration. And the centrepiece was, as I had hoped all along, the football scene.

2

Maestro

1953 was the year television came of age in England. We witnessed bits and pieces of the Everest adventure; my father glowed with nationalistic pride because of Sherpa Tenzing Norgay, as if Tenzing were a bona fide Indian (he wasn't at the time, although he became an Indian citizen later); he growled that the English media made much more fuss over Edmund Hillary and Colonel Hunt. The 'conquest' of Everest, cooed all the press, was a gorgeous gift to the Queen on the day of her coronation, which was beamed nationwide on television. The Australian cricket team, led by Lindsay Hassett, came over, and we watched gleefully as Len Hutton's England won back the Ashes. Before the series was over, I was besotted with Denis Compton and Keith Miller; it was the combination of their flamboyance on the cricket field and their debonair good looks.

At the end of that summer, we moved from Nottingham to Derby where my father took up a post at the Derbyshire Royal Infirmary. We left Nottingham amid tearful farewells. It was a Sunday and all our neighbours from the other flats at 22 Cavendish Crescent had assembled to see us off. My mother wept profusely, as she always did on such occasions.

I was no stranger to the pain of parting. Three years earlier, my mother, grandmother and I were seen off at the airport in Calcutta by our relatives. My mother was unable to stop crying but for some reason that particular farewell did not affect me in the same way; I was too excited by the prospect of my first trip in a plane – to Bombay, where we would catch the ship for Liverpool. I became upset not that day but the next when, fresh from a night's sleep at the Taj Hotel, we boarded the ship that would take us to Britain, a small Indian-owned vessel called the S.S. *Jal Jawahar*, and stood on the deck waiting to depart.

This time there was just my uncle – my mother's older, only brother whom I adored – to see us off. He stood on the quay dressed impeccably as always. Although he was six feet tall (unusually tall for a Bengali), as we gazed down at him from the ship, he looked a small, lonely figure. Then the ship started to move, almost imperceptibly, away from the quayside, and the murky, brown ribbon of water became a stream, then a canal, then a narrow river, and eventually as wide as the River Ganga (Ganges in English) that passes by Calcutta. I watched my uncle shrink till he was a mere blob, then almost nothing at all; and as the ship's resplendently uniformed band struck up one of the most sentimental but most beloved of Bengali patriotic songs, written by the poet-composer Dwijendra Lal Roy, and then followed this with the Indian national anthem, I heard my mother sobbing and at that moment I felt a blinding urge to leap, jump, fly across the ever-widening stretch of water back to the security of my uncle's arms. Unable to do this, I exploded into tears.

That Sunday in Nottingham, as our taxi drew away from the ivy-clad house which had been our home, did I feel the same pain? I can no longer remember. But I can still relive the loneliness that assaulted me during those first few weeks in Derby.

Perhaps to deflect this loneliness, this longing for Nottingham,
I sought out from among my possessions a book I had airily cast
aside till then. It was a boys' book of sports – I cannot remember
who gave it to me. Perhaps one of my adopted Bengali bachelor
dadas, or one of the other residents of the house we shared. Or
perhaps my mother had bought it for me, as a consolation. I had
glanced at it, but no more than that, for it did not look interesting. I was immersed in *The Wonder Book of Trains*.

In Derby, homesick for Nottingham and disconsolate, I opened
this book simply because it reminded me of the life I had just
abandoned. The opening paragraph in the editor's introduction
caught my attention. It spoke of the year of the coronation as
one that was most gratifying for English sports lovers. England
had recovered the Ashes; someone called Gordon Richards had at
last won the Derby; a British expedition had climbed Mount
Everest; Pegasus had won the FA Amateur Cup watched by one
hundred thousand people – 'One hundred thousand people to
watch an amateur game!' – the writer exclaimed. And a football
player by the name of Stanley Matthews had finally won his
winner's medal in the most glorious of Cup Finals. All these great
events, the editor promised, were covered in the book.

This last part caught my attention in particular for some
reason. Who was Stanley Matthews, what was the Cup Final, and
why was it so important (and for whom) that he should win a
medal? And why did the writer call him 'Maestro'?

By the beginning of the Christmas holidays I cannot say to
what extent my academic knowledge had been enhanced at the
new school; but thanks to that book, and further, feverish explo-
ration of the football pages of the *Manchester Guardian* (which,
despite my plea that we should keep the more flashy-looking
Daily Mirror, my father subscribed to, being a staunch supporter
of the Labour Party – for it was in the time of Clement Attlee's

leadership that India obtained independence), these questions were answered to my complete satisfaction.

Certain tableaux in that book were seared into my brain: a goalmouth scene, a goalkeeper's helpless, outstretched hands, in the far left a falling figure, in the foreground two men with triumphant, outstretched arms; two men raised aloft by their teammates, both clutching the handles of the trophy, the FA Cup; one of these two men with his back turned slightly towards the viewer, number seven on the shirt, receiving his medal from Princess Elizabeth – as she was for a few weeks more. Within days the names were as familiar as my cousins' names back in Calcutta. Within days I had looked up where Blackpool was on the map of Britain; within weeks I knew the name of every player in the team, and the positions they played. By Guy Fawkes Day or thereabouts, I knew the story of the 1953 FA Cup Final by heart; I knew the goal-by-goal score, Bolton 1–Blackpool 0, Bolton 1–Blackpool 1, Bolton 2–Blackpool 1, then half-time, then Bolton 3–Blackpool 1, and despair among the Blackpool supporters as the minutes rolled by, before Bolton 3–Blackpool 2, then miraculously Bolton 3–Blackpool 3, and with only minutes left, everyone expecting extra time, Bolton 3–Blackpool 4, and all the world (except Bolton) exploded in disbelief and delight, and so Stanley Matthews won his so elusive FA Cup winner's medal.

Football began to make sense. The hazy notions I had gathered the previous winter were dispelled and replaced by the first stirrings of what could be properly called footballing knowledge. In my case these were composed almost entirely of the facts and events and players of the 1953 FA Cup Final. And at the core lay fragments of a kind of magic-laden lore surrounding this man called Stanley Matthews.

That early autumn, without ever having seen the man in action – not on the playing field certainly, but not even as a flickering image on the television screen, nor even as a succession of those infuriatingly edited jump-cut motions on the newsreel we see in cinemas – but by way of my imagination constructing and reconstructing his moves as I read about the Cup Final, by way of my gazing intently at his pictures, by way of such subterfuge, Stanley Matthews displaced Denis Compton as my main idol; and, on the strength of that one match, that one match description, I became a fan of Blackpool Football Club.

In the meantime, there was the problem of coming to terms with Derby.

3

In the Baseball Ground

Kedleston Road where we came to live was as distinct from Cavendish Crescent as one could imagine. The latter had been a silent street, indeed the whole neighbourhood had been. Yet that quietness never made me uneasy. Cars would pass through but not many; they mostly belonged to the local residents, and there were just enough to produce a sense of life, of comings and goings. An unmenacing kind of silence.

In Derby, Kedleston Road was a busy road, a major bus route. Our part of the road was composed of a hotchpotch of houses, shops of the baker-butcher-greengrocer type, schools, and a few small offices, estate agents, solicitors and the like. Cavendish Crescent and its environs had been almost posh. Kedleston Road was merely nice, merely respectable.

We came to live in the first-floor flat at number 108, at an exuberant part of the road. In contrast, Cavendish Crescent had seemed almost stately, a bit too mannered. Close by were a girls' grammar school, Parkfield Cedars, and a secondary modern called Sturgess School. Twice each weekday, the stretch in front of our house would be rent by a cacophony of chatter and shouts and laughter as students passed by. My mother rejoiced in this noisy cheerfulness – it almost reminded her of the swarming streets of Calcutta. Each afternoon, she would poke her head out of the kitchen window overlooking the road and watch the throngs go by.

She became much more light-hearted after we came to Derby. In Nottingham there were times – when she was not busy with household chores or running errands or there were no guests – when the greyness and gloom of a wintry Sunday afternoon, and the general, deserted air of the street in front would affect her intensely. She would sit on the window seat which looked out onto the lawn, close her eyes and sing Tagore's *Rabindra-sangeet*. She would select ones that matched the atmosphere without and her mood within – invariably slow, melancholic song poems like the monsoon season song which in Tagore's *Gitanjali* (Song Offerings) – the volume that had won him the Nobel prize back in 1913 – begins, in English, with the line 'Clouds Heap upon Clouds and It Darkens'. Then she would start to cry, sick with longing for her home in Calcutta.

My mother was immensely gifted musically. In Calcutta, she had received the title of *Geetasree* meaning, roughly, one who had achieved the highest mastery of music, at the age of thirteen. She had made many recordings and, before her marriage (and for a while after), she sang on All India Radio.

In Derby, England appeared a little less grey to her. She would sing while cooking, not casually but seriously, as if in front of an audience; and not just *Rabindra-sangeet* but songs from popular Hindi movies, by K. L. Saigal, one of her favourites, or one of M. S. Subhalakshmi's *bhajans* (devotional songs) from the hit film *Meera*. When the weather was warm and the kitchen window was up, unfamiliar strains in unfamiliar languages would drift down to the road below, and surprised pedestrians would glance up out of curiosity. Or she would sing her favourite English and American songs. Once, entering the front door from the streets, I heard the sounds and words of Slim Whitman's 'Rose Marie' loud and crystal clear descend from the kitchen window.

Our landlord, Mr Walter Amos – tall and craggily handsome 'in a Gary Cooper sort of way' according to my admiring mother – lived with his wife, daughter Pauline and son Bob on the first floor. He worked as a porter at the Derbyshire Royal Infirmary; this posed an unfamiliar social dilemma for my father the first time he ran into Mr Amos in the hospital. Here was my father, small, dapper, a herring-bone-three-piece-suited surgeon who commanded authority, the nurses' deference, and the patients' anxiety-laden adoration. And there was his landlord, in his dark blue porter's uniform, possibly pushing a trolley or some such thing down the hospital corridor. My father was very definitely confused (as I overheard him say to my mother) as he searched for the appropriate demeanour to adopt, response to make, script to construct, for this novel situation.

My mother was likewise discomfited when, returning home by bus after shopping in town, she saw that the uniformed conductress collecting fares was Mrs Amos. In the *bhadrolok* world my parents inhabited – in Bengali this means, literally, 'gentleman', but used more broadly to refer to people of the upper middle-class, well-educated, Bengali elite – bus conductors and railway ticket collectors, postmen and milkmen played definite roles and occupied well-defined places in one's life; they performed essential but intellectually undemanding services, wore rough-textured or relatively rude clothes, and were largely faceless, nameless beings. My parents, liberal and enlightened though they were, belonged to this universe. Thus, one did not expect that the bus conductor about to collect a fare was one's landlady, with whom one shared a house.

My parents' collective disorientation was further exacerbated by the fact that the landlord-porter and landlady-conductress owned a car, a gleaming, new, dark blue Vauxhall Velox, whereas they did not. So every morning, while the impeccably suited surgeon caught the bus to the hospital, the uniformed porter and the uniformed bus conductress would get into their car and drive off to work.

Then there was Pauline, their daughter. Slim, tall (to my eight-year-old perception, at least), blonde, twenty perhaps or twenty-one, and (to me) wondrously beautiful. I was smitten the first day we met. I took every opportunity to run into her, sometimes in the hallway leading out to the front door or else on the front steps outside, or even in the passageway across from the first-floor landing in front of the bathroom we all shared. If I spotted her out in the back garden tending to Flash, the Amoses' Alsatian dog, I would dash down the stairs two steps at a time and then saunter out into the garden, so casually, on the pretext that I wanted to play with the dog.

One evening, stopping by the Amoses' kitchen, I came upon Pauline in a shoulderless evening gown. She was going to a dance and waiting for her escort. The image of her golden hair swept back and up in that sleek, unfamiliar way, the curves of her bare shoulders and the faint parting of her breasts at the décolletage stayed with me that whole evening. It may have even disturbed my boyish equanimity for this was not the vision of Pauline I cherished.

But then, as I learned very soon, she was to be engaged – to a fellow called Stanley. *Stanley!* My realization that there was something serious going on between them came one evening when I went downstairs to watch a television programme in the Amoses' living room. There they were, Pauline and Stanley, lying stretched out, entwined, on the long sofa. Embarrassed, I averted my gaze,

Mr and Mrs Amos.

and watched the whole show sitting on a pouffe in front of the screen, with my back to the sofa. All the time I sat there I was intensely and miserably aware of their unseen but definitely felt presence. As I stared at the disembodied images, only a part of my mind was on the screen. I would hear Pauline laugh – a cooing, low-throated, unfamiliar sound. For long moments there would be total silence and I thought they must then be kissing. I heard murmurs, mostly her voice, low and silky and naughty. I was hugely disturbed.

Beyond home lay the neighbourhood; and beyond that lay school. St Philomena's Convent School, to be precise, known simply as Convent School.

When we first came to England, to Nottingham, my parents decided that I should go to a Catholic school. It was a wholly artless decision. Had we been in Calcutta, I would have attended – as my mother, her brother and cousins had – one of the 'English Medium' schools, which were located mostly in the elegant *sahib para*, a colloquial Bengali term used to refer to the locality in Calcutta where British *sahibs* and their wives, *memsahibs*, had lived before Indian independence. I would have probably gone to St Xavier's, a Jesuit institution where my father had attended college before going on to medical school. My mother's school had been Loreto House, run by nuns. So it seemed perfectly obvious to her (though perhaps less so to my father) that I would go to a Catholic school in England. She took this to be axiomatic.

St Philomena's, my new school, as I discovered in progressively extending my zone of familiarity, was not too far from our house once one knew the back streets. To get there on foot all I needed to do was make my way down Kedleston Road towards town, to Five Lamps, the big roundabout from where five roads radiated out, cross to the road opposite, up a few dozen yards past the car showroom where I would pause to admire the low-slung, gleaming, bright-red Triumph TR2 (that no one seemed to want to buy), then turn into a side street on which stood the Children's Hospital my father visited on Friday afternoons to tend to young, recalcitrant ears, noses and throats, then a few turns right, left, and right again, and I would reach my school.

The entrance was a plain, blue wooden door underneath some kind of brick archway, the only relief in the long, unprepossessing wall. That first day, a passer-by seeing the door opened by a nun to admit us could have easily imagined that fifty years ago, instead of a small eight- or nine-year-old, brown-complexioned boy standing there, there would have been a young, pale-skinned, wisp of a teenage girl waiting to be admitted as a novice.

The only suggestion that the place was anything other than a nunnery was the cacophony of high-pitched voices, shrill cries and laughter, the rapid-fire clattering of shoes on cement, muffled thumps of small rubber balls rebounding against the wall – the archetypal, unmistakable sound of a playground, that would erupt abruptly from within at certain times of the day.

At first, I was happy enough at Convent School. I had never found it hard to make friends, and the colour of my skin, the strangeness of my first name and the place of my origin lent me, perhaps, an aura of the unusual, if not of outright exotica, which always provoked curiosity among other boys and girls as well as their parents.

Quickly, I befriended a boy whose slightly rotund girth was well matched by the round, metal-rimmed, National Health prescription glasses he wore. Graham Dean, I discovered, lived quite close to me, on Wheeldon Avenue, leading just off Kedleston Road a dozen yards from our house.

For the first time I had found someone with whom I could talk football. But Graham had no interest in Stanley Matthews, and certainly none in Blackpool. How could he even like Matthews when his hero was Tom Finney – a player of whom I had recently become aware? So did he support Finney's team, Preston North End? He did not. His teams were Wolverhampton Wanderers and Derby County – the Wolves and the Rams. I think this was when I faced my first great philosophical conundrum. How could someone support two teams? How could one be loyal to the Wolves *and* the Rams? For Graham this was clearly no problem – indeed, I was even more perplexed when he said he also supported Aberdeen!

I may have talked about this dilemma with Graham or one of my other band of steadily growing friends – I cannot recall. But I certainly came to a kind of rationalization along the following lines. Derby County was the town's local team. It was like family – one is bound to it by blood ties. Whereas the 'other team', whichever it was, was like a best friend. There was no problem in loving a relative and a friend; they were two different kinds of love. As for a third team – like Graham's Aberdeen – well, that was more a kind of fascination than love or passion, the fascination one has with a distant place or relative across the seas. Aberdeen was in Scotland, after all – it was not an English team.

This meant that I, too, could become a Derby County supporter without feeling guilty. There remained one niggling thought. What if Blackpool were to play Derby? For the moment I could almost safely put that question aside, because Derby County had been relegated the last season to the Second Division, while Blackpool was still a powerhouse in the First. There was, of course, always the possibility of their meeting one another in an FA cup-tie. But there seemed no point in worrying about that. I would have to deal with it if and when it occurred.

A new world had opened up, a new source of knowledge. Since my father was keeping the *Derby Evening Telegraph*, I buried myself in its back pages, and within a few days of intense reading

I was thoroughly familiar with the names and faces of the Derby County players. I even began to refer to them casually, affectionately, as 'the Rams', as if I had known them all my life.

Sadly, I realized that there was none in the team that could compare with the Blackpool team, no genius to match Matthews, no goal scorers with the 'speed, dash and verve' (according to the words of my precious book of sports) of Blackpool's centre forward, the 'other' Stanley – Stanley Mortensen (and certainly no one as handsome as him!) – or (according to a newspaper article I read) of Allan Brown who had made the winning strike against Arsenal in the quarter-final last year and simultaneously broke his leg, no one as commanding in defence (so my book said) as the Blackpool captain Harry Johnston, no one with the guile of inside forward 'little' Ernie Taylor (he was always described as 'little', almost like 'Little John', Robin Hood's pal). There was not even anyone in the Rams team who had played for England – or any other country for that matter. No, the Rams were a decidedly ordinary team. Graham's father, Mr Dean, who seemed to take to me, would often speak of 'that team' of just a few years ago, the team that had won the FA Cup just after the Second World War. The *Derby Evening Telegraph*, in the midst of its gloomy ruminations, would also write wistfully of 'that' team. 'That' team had had Raich Carter, who was possessed of genius (I gathered) and had partnered Matthews in the England line-up; and 'that' team had had Peter Doherty who had formed, with Raich Carter (so I gathered) the best inside forward pair in the country. I heard of men who had played for England those days, names that cropped up again and again whenever anyone spoke or wrote of 'that' team and its successors in the years that followed the war: Carter and Bert Mozley and Tim Ward and Johnny Morris – now, the last-named interested me, for here was a connection between Blackpool and

Derby County: Morris had played for Manchester United against Blackpool in the 1948 FA Cup Final (the 'greatest Cup Final ever' – so I read somewhere), which Blackpool had lost. I heard of Billy Steel who played for Scotland.

But they were all gone: Mr Dean mourned, the *Telegraph* mourned, everyone I came into contact with and who cared for the Rams mourned, and I could only share their regret.

My network of footballing knowledge was steadily growing, but still only in my imagination. I had been comforted by the fact that Graham had never actually seen the Wolves play; but he had at least seen Tom Finney in action, the season before, when Preston came to play Derby. He had seen Derby County – several times. Whereas I had yet to witness a real game played by adult players. This flaw in my character was corrected quite by accident one Saturday afternoon; it must have been a month or two after we arrived in Derby. My parents, perhaps gaining confidence in our new neighbourhood, allowed me to wander about and go beyond the range of their Indian over-anxious eyes and so I began to happily explore the length of Kedleston Road, the streets that led off it, the places they led to.

Thus it was that one Saturday, some time after lunch, not finding Graham to play with, nor the boy I had befriended from next door, Harold Heldrich, that I wandered alone down Cowley Street. Graham's uncle, his father's brother, had a newsagent's somewhere down that street he had told me, and perhaps it was just to locate this shop that I chose to go in that direction.

I found Dean's Newsagents, paused to inspect it, then went by it, passed a barber's shop, onto another street called (I saw) Mackworth Road, and suddenly came upon a stretch of green. A park. I would soon learn that this was the local Recreation Ground – 'the Rec'. It lay on both sides of the road. In fact, on one side, it was not a park at all, more of a playground, for I could see swings and seesaws, but the ground itself was a mixture of cindery gravel, cement and grass that was rather mean-looking and sparse. A child falling off a swing here could get badly hurt.

What was really interesting was the other part, on the opposite side of the road, for this had real grass. In fact, most of it was taken up with a large football field with goalposts which, I was thrilled to see, were draped with nets, like the ones I saw in my precious sports book. And a game was about to begin!

Perhaps I summoned up enough courage to ask one of the men standing nearby the names of the teams. I learned that the home team was called West End. That was all I was told, but it was all that mattered. The players were already on the pitch, kicking footballs about, preparing for the kick-off. There was quite a large gathering of spectators, and their presence, and the fact that many of them seemed to be on close terms with one or another of the West End players, gave the whole scene a delightful air of intimacy. I took a deep breath. I could see myself being here on many future Saturday afternoons.

Standing on the goal line, and noting the goalkeepers' distinctive, polo-neck jerseys, I was taken aback by the proximity of these massive men slip-sliding in a fast accumulating mud. The only sound of football I was actually familiar with was the undulating roar of invisible, mass crowds heard on Saturday afternoon broadcasts on BBC radio. I could never have guessed how physical the game was when real men played it, the sweat that flowed freely down their faces, the phlegm they were constantly spitting, the frequent expulsion of nose stuff; I could never have guessed how it could sound close up, the thuds of leather on leather, the grunts of pain when body met body, the curses, the shouts, the perpetual instructions that flowed from one to another, the anxious urgency in their voices in moments of crisis. I was startled by the obscenities that rent the air, not just by the players but also the spectators; I was a bit frightened by the venom in their voices – as the man next to me yelled 'fucking bastard' at an opposition player who had brought down the West End centre forward with a huge and vicious lunge near where I stood. The culprit was so near he must have heard, but he seemed merely amused for he flashed a quick grin in our general direction before moving away. This was the day I realized that football did something to men, even the mildest-mannered of them, like the cloth-capped, raincoated, bifocalled little man standing nearby, who smiled at me, and patted my head cheerfully one moment and snarled at the opposition the next. I was as enthralled listening to the spectators and watching their ever-changing expressions as I was with the match itself.

That game was but an aperitif. Not long after, I persuaded my father to take me to the Baseball Ground to watch Derby play.

My father's interest in football was rather vague. Let me explain. I was aware even then that in Calcutta, there were two great rival teams named East Bengal and Mohun Bagan. Later, I came to understand this mutual hostility in more British terms: this was no ordinary rivalry between clubs from the same city – not the kind of rivalry between Manchester United and Manchester City, or between Liverpool and Everton. It was more ferocious – the Glasgow Rangers–Glasgow Celtic kind of hostility, not sectarian as in their case, but rooted in fundamental, region-based affinities. The supporters of East Bengal were people whose ancestral homes, towns and villages were in East Bengal, which had become a part of Pakistan after India won its independence, while Mohun Bagan was a club of the original inhabitants of Calcutta itself. If Rangers–Celtic games brought out the passions of religious bigotry between Catholics and Protestants, the East Bengal–Mohun Bagan matches were battles between the natives of Calcutta – the *Kolkatyas* – and the migrants from East Bengal, the *Bangals*. On the playing fields of the *Maidan*, the great stretch of green in Calcutta where the eminences of the British Raj use to 'take the air', where these teams held their matches, there was no love lost between *Kolkatyas* and *Bangals*. Outside the football ground, there may not have been mutual hostility, but they found each other's habits, manners and lifestyles strange, and objects of derision. They scarcely spoke the same kind of Bengali.

My families – on both my mother's and father's sides – were from East Bengal. My mother's ancestral home was in Dhaka, formerly anglicized to 'Dacca', now capital of the nation of Bangladesh; my father's ancestral home was in the district of Barisal. And so both families were, automatically, East Bengal supporters. My father's interest was, thus, of an obligatory sort. If he had actually gone to watch East Bengal play, I was not aware of it.

But he was a kindly, dutiful father and so, however reluctantly, he took me to the Baseball Ground one Saturday. I did not have a black-and-white scarf as I had seen others wear, nor did I possess a rattle. I wore the closest garment I had to the Rams' colours, a very deep blue windcheater and a matching woollen cap which I hoped would be mistaken for black. I was acutely conscious of the inadequacy of my attire and asked my mother to buy or knit me a black-and-white scarf. She promised me something better: she said that by Christmas or at the latest the New Year, I would have a black, woollen, zip-up cardigan with white collars and white cuffs.

We went by bus and alighted somewhere near the ground. We became a part of a slowly thickening crowd moving along entirely unfamiliar streets, unbroken rows of murky, red-brick, clone-like houses, no garden in front, no enclosures of any sort, no shrubs, nothing to break the monotony of dull red brick and lace curtains. And above there were the chimneys; row upon cheerless row of them, in every direction I could see as I gazed up, placed almost identically, three, four or even five to a stack, hundreds of them, it seemed, huddled into small groups. They reminded me of crows in Calcutta bunched together on telegraph wires and the tops of walls, except that the crows cawed in raucous union, while these soot-caked sentinels emitted in collective silence dirty trickles of smoke.

There would be days later when I would walk through these streets and others like them. In the daytime, on weekdays, these streets would be uncannily, deathly quiet, broken only by the sound of sporadic footfalls or the whirring of the odd bicycle. There would not be many cars in these parts, and if the bus route lay a small distance away the sounds of modern technology were relatively scarce.

But that day, an hour before kick-off, it was different. The houses still looked impassive, with no life in them; perhaps they all shut themselves off when Saturday came from the thumping and clatter of boots and shoes on the pavement, and the murmur that steadily grew as the throng increased, fans turning one corner and then another, people appearing from all sides, so that after a while you were afraid to stop, you let yourself be carried along by this vast, inexorable flow of humanity in black-and-white.

And I was part of that throng! That first day, my first visit to a professional football match, I understood what it was to belong.

Finally, we arrived at the Baseball Ground. I had not known quite what to expect. As we slid, one by one, through the narrow turnstile, the stands looked older, more run down, than the mental image I had carried from the pictures in the *Derby Evening Telegraph*. We came out onto the terrace very near the top, from which we had a splendid view of the whole ground, but that was because the stadium was still relatively empty. I discovered that this hitherto mysterious thing called 'the terraces' was really a succession of very broad strips of concrete descending like a broad staircase from the back to the front. It reminded me of cinemas that sloped down from the rear.

We walked down to the front, which was where all the young-sters and smaller adults stood so as to see clearly. Reaching the bottom of the terraces I discovered I was just tall enough for my head to be above the wall separating the terraces from the pitch itself. My head was literally at ground level.

I cannot recall the visiting team. Perhaps it was Birmingham City, for there is an association in my mind between that first time at the Baseball Ground and an event that would happen a few days later at Wembley, and embedded in that association is the image of the Birmingham goalkeeper, Gilbert Merrick.

We stood there, patiently spinning out the time before the game began, breathing in cold air, expelling smoke and stamping our feet to keep warm. When the game finally began, I had scarcely any sensation in my toes except a gnawing, numbing pain – like hunger pangs, but in the feet. I had known this pain before – it happened whenever I was exposed to prolonged cold, as when I would play in the park.

But that hardly mattered now. I knew first hand the genteel, contemplative sound of cricket. Before watching the match at the Rec, the only sound of football I knew was what I had heard sit-ting on a pouffe listening to the transmitted and filtered roar of unseen spectators during BBC radio broadcasts of matches, superimposed sometimes by the sound of the whirring of a thou-sand rattles. Now, I looked about me greedily, exultantly, not wanting to miss any sight or sound.

Almost deserted when we first arrived, the terraces gradually, almost imperceptibly, became blotched with clusters of people here and there; then there were more clusters, and then the clusters grew in size, like colonies of some mysterious organism, till they interpenetrated one another so that, at kick-off, I could see just one monolithic mass of humanity, the dull, sickly pallor of coats, windcheaters and raincoats broken and brightened only by splashes of blacks and whites from scarves, caps and rosettes. Not a single square foot of the terrace remained unoccupied, not a single strip of concrete could be seen. And this for a team that had just been relegated to the Second Division! What had it been like in their glory days – when they had had 'that' team?

What struck me was how good humoured they all were in spite of, but not oblivious to, the cold. Sometimes a wave of laughter would break out somewhere as someone made a ribald sally. Then, as the teams suddenly materialized from out of some dark cavern on the other side, they all gave vent, all fifteen, sixteen, twenty thousand of them, to a collective roar, the sound I had heard on the radio but vastly more terrifying in reality – because I was part of it. I, too, yelled in my squeaky nine-year-old voice.

I was as much attracted by the sound as by the game itself: when a promising Derby move began, the low, humdrum murmur would start to rise in pitch like the whistle and the gush of an approaching train and, with the imminence of a goal, swell in intensity and explode into a roar and then, if it all came to naught, the roar would subside suddenly to a disappointed, frustrated growl. And throughout the match, there was the perpetual, raucous, nerve-grinding, encouraging clamour of furiously whirling rattles.

The match began as if in a dream. In the first few minutes after the players entered the field, as my eyes devoured the scene – of one player limbering up here, another sprinting short bursts there, a couple of them exchanging rapid-fire passes, a goalkeeper (wearing a green polo-neck jersey!) fielding a succession of volleys launched at him from different directions – I felt a strange sensation course through me.

It was the sensation of recognition, on being confronted in the flesh and blood by those you have only seen in photographic images and in your imagination – a sensation of pleasure rather than ecstasy. Even though these Rams players were not national celebrities (in modern language, there were no superstars, not even stars), a few were widely respected, one had played for England, and all were household names in Derby itself. They were the stuff of the daily back pages of the *Derby Evening Telegraph*.

It was the sensation of confirmation that those you were led to believe existed really did exist, they really did resemble their images lodged somewhere in the library of one's mind.

It was also the sensation of small surprises and disappointments and adjustments to those stored images, as certain assumptions that were part of those images were not met exactly by the reality – that this centre forward was much smaller, that halfback less handsome, this winger had a sallower skin than what the images said.

The merging of these sensations can neither be named nor described adequately – just as one cannot ever describe one's hunger pangs. One can only experience this sensation and recall and re-experience it later.

Derby lost the match four goals to two, but long before the match ended I had ceased to care: just after half-time, as the spectators settled down again and play resumed, I discovered to my chagrin that I needed to pee. I might have been able to pass between those tightly packed bodies out to where the lavatories were, but I was afraid that if I vacated my precious spot I would never recover it. The void created would be filled immediately.

Moreover, besides losing my place and not being able to see the rest of the match from behind those massive bodies at the back of the terrace, I would also lose sight of my father and would never be able to return home.

So I stayed where I was. I said nothing to my father who was a few feet away and behind me; there was nothing he could do. As my discomfort increased, I thought briefly and in desperation of the possibility that if I did manage to squeeze my way out, the grown-ups would take pity on me and hand me down above their heads, one man to another from the rear to the front, the way I had seen one small boy transferred to the front at the start of the game. But this did not guarantee that I would return to where I was, or that I would not lose sight of my father. After all, he was a small man. In despair, I rejected this idea.

So, as the game wound its way through the second half to another Derby defeat, I watched the game with unseeing eyes. My mind was committed to the task of controlling my will and my bladder. My whole body was taut with the effort. I wondered, in case I wet my pants, whether the people around me would notice – and wished I had worn my navy blue mackintosh which at least came down to just below the knee instead of my thigh-length windcheater. At one point near the very end of the match, as the crowd roared instinctively but with no real hope at the (false) prospect of a third Derby goal, the cold, the urge to relieve myself, and the effort at self-control brought tears to my eyes. In Nottingham, I had once been unable to fall asleep; counting sheep had not helped. My father had suggested that I should imagine the prayer room on the rooftop terrace of our joint family home in Calcutta, and of the clay images of the various goddesses and gods – Kali, Lakshmi, the elephant god, Ganesh, and Saraswati – that stood there in a little altar, and where one of my uncles – my father's second older brother –

offered his twice-daily prayers, *puja*. My father had said that thinking about those images would calm my mind and I would be able to sleep.

I now thought once more of that prayer room – what I remembered of it – and I constructed the painted images in my mind. It had not helped before, it had not put me to sleep then, but it seemed to help this time for the effort of imagining, of remembering, distracted me, for a short while at least, from the shrill pain in my groin.

Eventually, the game ended, the Rams beaten. Scarcely aware of anything else, I was able to make my way to the lavatories through a disconsolate, dispersing crowd. On the bus, while our fellow passengers were reliving and reconstructing the game, there was not much I could remember of the second half. I had to wait till later, and the evening newspaper, to know what had actually transpired on the pitch after half-time.

4

Hungarian Rhapsody

While we were learning English history in class one late November afternoon in 1953, English history of another kind was being made at Wembley Stadium.

I never ever saw a film of the whole match between England and Hungary, only fragments, clips shown on television and on the newsreel at cinemas. What I saw of the game were rather like lightning strikes, jagged, momentarily blinding, things that just happened and were then gone, leaving after-images, as lightning does, of passes and footwork and shots on goal and ballet-like grace on the one hand, and frozen postures, glacial faces on the other. England – the football team and the footballing nation – were left in a state of stupor, and the newspaper columnists struggled for the right language, right demeanour, to give expression to their emotions and incredulity at what they had witnessed.

The next day I bought as many different newspapers as I could. The score, England 3–Hungary 6, scarcely said anything. It was not just (I read) that England had been beaten on its own soil for the first ever time by a foreign team; it was not that they had been thrashed; it was the manner in which they had been thrashed.

Again and again, I read in the papers, heard on the radio, and finally saw on television the third goal by Ferenc Puskás in which he dragged back the ball with the underside of his left boot away from Billy Wright's lunge and in that same move hit it high into the net, leaving Wright sprawled helplessly on his backside on the hallowed Wembley turf. And the goalkeeper, Gilbert Merrick, bothered and bewildered, could only look on in despair. The humiliation of one team captain by another. I read about, and could imagine in my mind, the first goal by the Hungarian centre forward Nándor Hidegkuti, inside the first minute before England had scarcely moved. I saw on the newsreel the last Hungarian goal by Hidegkuti, a kind of contemplative, arrogant volley from a Puskás pass. The camera was behind the net and I saw Merrick transfixed, helpless and hopeless.

It was not just that England was demolished in a football match, someone said, but that a glorious myth, the myth of English invincibility as a people and a nation, was destroyed in those ninety brief minutes. Not since William the Conqueror a thousand years before, said someone, had England been so crushingly overwhelmed on its own soil. What Hitler could not do in the Blitz, Ferenc Puskás and his teammates had done. If the British Empire was made on the playing fields of Eton, wrote another, then as surely it was unmade on the football field of Wembley that November afternoon.

I was as devastated as everyone else. Just as I had become a Blackpool supporter and a Derby County supporter, I had become an England supporter. My still sketchy knowledge of English football history had led me to believe in England's superiority in world football. After all, the English had invented the sport, they had bestowed it upon the world. I had been led to believe in England's invincibility on her own soil.

More vitally for me, this England team had four of my

Blackpool heroes playing that day : Harry Johnston at centre half, and the trio of Stanley Matthews, ('little') Ernie Taylor and Stanley Mortensen in the forward line. My one consolation was that my two main heroes accounted for themselves respectably. Mortensen created one of England's goals and scored their second; Matthews (according to the reports) was blameless – he was one of the better players on the English side that afternoon. Poor Harry Johnston, Blackpool's usually dependable, rocklike captain was quite embarrassed by Hidegkuti. And I never heard a word about Ernie Taylor.

It was a sour turn for what had otherwise been a good year for English heroes.

At the end of May, the whole of the British Isles woke one morning to the same picture on the front page of every newspaper: a Nepali man called Tenzing Norkay, his swarthy, beaming face barely visible below dark, heavy snow goggles, standing almost cockily on top of Mount Everest, holding aloft a flagstaff on which we could discern the Indian tricolour flag and the Union Jack. The word 'sherpa' entered the English language. In my school (and no doubt others) my geography teacher hastily looked up Nepal on the world map. The sun had not yet set on the British Empire!

My parents – my father in particular – and all my Bengali *dadas* surveyed the national euphoria with mixed emotions. They could not quite suppress their excitement. Yet, within the confines of our living room, they all sulked like small children as if their most precious toy had been taken from them.

They ranted and raved because Tenzing, a 'mere' Nepali sherpa, a mountain guide, a superior kind of coolie (in British eyes, so they said in our living room) had become (so they thought) an inconvenient aside, an embarrassment that sullied British celebrations. It was a British triumph, said the newspapers, said the radio, said television. Never mind that the two who finally reached the summit were a New Zealander and a Nepali. Edmund Hillary was, after all, a native of a loyal Dominion nation whose flag still had the Union Jack in inset. So the British adopted him as one of their own. It was all about Hillary, one of our Bengali bachelors angrily stuttered. (No one admitted something that I came to realize later: that the Indians were as guilty, because they claimed Tenzing as one of their own.)

My father had other, more emotive, more private misgivings. For him, Everest was like a precious personal or family possession. His family – my patrilineal family – had strong Nepali connections: my father's older brother was, and had been for a long time, the royal physician – physician to the Nepali royal family, and was a long-time resident of Kathmandu. Everest had captivated my father ever since the first time he had visited Kathmandu in 1942. When the latest Everest expedition was announced, he would pore over guidebooks. He learned the strange names of its lesser peaks and passed them on to us. There could not have been many housewives or small boys outside Nepal who could talk about North Col and South Col as my mother and I could. He learned its history and that of its victims, those who had died on its slopes. The tragedy of Mallory gripped him, and he relished the story of the doomed mountaineer who when asked why he wanted to climb Everest had answered: 'Because it is there.'

My father knew bits and pieces of the history of the mountain before it was called Everest, when it was known by cryptic code letters. He would fret that this mountain that had arisen in his part of the world should be named after an Englishman. I heard from him about a nineteenth-century Bengali, Radhanath Sikdar, who (my father said, darkly) was thought to have calculated the height of Everest when it was called, simply, XV. It should have been named Mount Sikdar, my father said, rather than after Sir George Everest.

Quite irrationally, I realized even then, my father would poke fun about a British Isles that could boast only of what he called 'puny hillocks'. He would say, mockingly, that they made mountains out of British molehills. He took jingoistic comfort that 'we' of the Indian subcontinent possessed Everest and Kanchanjunga, and 'they' had only Ben Nevis and Snowdon.

And after Everest had been climbed, my father could only look askance as the British celebrated. He was forced to admit that psychologically Everest had become 'theirs' as geographically it was 'ours'. The British had returned in triumph to lay claim once again to a chunk of 'our' homeland.

When England lost to Hungary, in our living room in the Kedleston Road flat, I seemed once more to be among the enemies. While the whole of England mourned, my father and our Bengali friends who would spend their weekends with us as they had done in Nottingham gloated. And, of course, they teased me – for in their eyes I was England's ambassador in their little world.

I was resigned to their jibes – it was not a new experience for me. By now I had come to believe that though not English born I was English bred. I was taking my Englishness for granted. And so when England succeeded I felt excited and pleased. If they failed I was depressed.

I was not indifferent to India. In fact, I was quite sure I loved her. But I found this hostility amongst the Bengalis towards the English upsetting, incomprehensible. It was ever-present, if not continuous or unending, and every now and then it would erupt. I would overhear snatches of rude remarks or snide comments, suddenly, in the midst of chatter, laughter, the clatter of crockery, the clinking of cutlery, the noise of dishes being washed, the sound of a *Rabindra-sangeet* on the gramophone, or my mother bursting impetuously into a much-loved Hindi film song.

When that happened, my sense of bonhomie would immediately evaporate. I would feel confused.

The Hungarian episode puzzled me in another way. I could understand if it had been India beating England, as they had done in the cricket test match in Madras the winter before, when Vinoo Mankad, the Indian all-rounder, took eight wickets in an innings. But why were they so happy about Hungary? What was Hungary to India?

It was only many years later that I would come upon the answer in a line I read somewhere: 'We think of our enemy's enemy as our friend.'

The peculiar, ambivalent relationship between India and England would rear its head in the most unexpected ways. I had started collecting stamps while in Nottingham, and had been caught quickly by the collector's obsession, the thrill of acquisition for the sake of acquisition. I no longer needed to fret on rainy days, for I could always turn to my stamp album with its beautiful, bottle-green, gold-bordered hard cover and flip its loose-leaf pages. At the top of each page was the country's name, the name of its capital and the country's population. I would mouth these names silently and savour the strangeness of their sounds: Belgian Congo, British Honduras, Eire, Gold Coast, Mauritius, Seychelles, Tonga, Zanzibar, Dutch This, French That. The very names soon became old friends. They came in pairs – country and capital: Argentina/Buenos Aires, Australia/Canberra, Brazil/Rio de Janeiro, Canada/Ottawa, Ceylon/Colombo, Hungary/Budapest, Peru/Lima, Portugal/Lisbon, Uruguay/Montevideo.

My perception of the world was shaped by this collection. It was through my stamps I came to know Hungary long before Puskás and Hidegkuti and Czibor and Guyala Grosics became household names. I admired Hungary because they issued stupendously magnificent, large and varied stamps, some even diamond-shaped; small works of art in themselves. I had no doubt that Hungary was an important land because of the beauty of its stamps!

My most treasured set, however, was the first day cover for the Queen's coronation posted to me from London by one of my Bengali *dadas*. There it lay, poised, composed, lightly hinged so that it would not get damaged, the whole envelope with my name written in bold, purple-inked handwriting, enjoying an entire page of the 'Great Britain' section for itself. Next in pride of place was another set of first day issues from the Vatican, commemorating the installation of the most recent pope. My father had acquired them when he was living in Rome. But apart from these two sets, the large Hungarian stamps, inscribed 'Magyar', showing cyclists and athletes in bright red and green and orange were my favourites.

My confusion about Anglo-Indian relations was hugely precipitated the evening I showed my father my most recent acquisitions, a set of twelve stamps I had bought that day from a small stamps shop just off Sadler Gate, not far from Derby Public Library. They were Indian stamps; not particularly beautiful, for all they displayed were the heads of George V and George VI. I was certain my father would be pleased by my interest in India.

I was horribly wrong! When I proudly showed him the page on which I had carefully mounted the stamps, his olive complexion turned dark and he angrily tore off the stamps one by one leaving in their wake only the dirty-looking hinges, like ugly scar marks.

I was devastated, stunned, bewildered, in tears. I wanted an explanation.

The British, my father said, had ruled over India for two hundred years. These stamps were of British India, not Independent India. They were reminders of those times. Therefore, they were worthless.

More gently my mother explained. That was when I properly grasped for the first time that India had become an independent nation after I was born. I was a child of British India.

5

Race and Other Relations

When we first arrived in England, it did not take me long to discover that the English were not good at pronouncing foreign-sounding names. Few people called me by my full first name; they would shorten it to 'Brata' or 'Brati', or more humorously 'Brat'. They preferred my nickname, 'Poupeé', given to me by my maternal uncle, my mother's older brother. They even had difficulty with my mother's name, Protima; they wanted to call her (and some did) Petulia (which I thought was just as complicated). As for Satyabrata, my father's first name, they did not even begin to pronounce it. Even Dasgupta was problematic. And so, in disgust, my father shortened it to 'Gupta'. For the whole of the rest of our collective life in England, my father and I became, to all intents and purposes, 'S. D. Gupta'.

My father insisted that this was not some biological inability on the part of the English to pronounce Asian names and words but rather their arrogant disinclination to do so. This was why, he claimed, that the British in India changed place names at will – why 'Kolkata' became 'Calcutta', 'Ganga' was turned into 'Ganges' and 'Dhaka' into 'Dacca', 'Kanya Kumari' became 'Cape

Comorin', and 'Vishakapatnam' was transformed into 'Vizag'. And Mihir-*da* agreed with my father.

Of all the Bengalis who drifted in and out of our lives in Nottingham and Derby, Mihir Sen was the most prominent and the closest to us. He was the Indian test wicketkeeper Probir Sen's younger brother and so an old acquaintance, through inter-family ties, of my mother. I called him Mihir-*da*, short for Mihir *dada*. He lived in Derby where he was employed by International Combustion, a boiler-manufacturing company with operations in Calcutta and elsewhere in India. He was short, slightly squat, with a deceptively earnest face, and he would gaze at you owlishly through thick-framed glasses. He had a stammer that would get worse when he was excited, which was very often. From fragments of overheard conversation between Mihir-*da* and my mother – who was 'Protima-*di*' (short for *didi*) to him – I inferred that he was something of a ladies'man. I would some-times see my mother laughing uncontrollably as she listened to anecdotes of his girl-chasing antics.

Of course I was greatly attracted to Mihir-*da* from the first day I met him because of his cricketing connections. He regaled me with stories of Indian cricket players past and present whom he knew personally; and of the times when Denis Compton and other English cricketers stationed in India during the war came to dinner at their family home in Calcutta, and when, after meals, someone would sing 'Tipperary' or 'Lili Marlene'. Mihir-*da*'s singing voice was as tuneless as they come, but he would blithely launch into these songs and I learned them from him. So strong is the association in my mind between these two songs and Mihir-*da* that years later, watching *Judgment at Nuremberg* in a Calcutta cinema and hearing 'Lili Marlene' on the soundtrack, I was transported back to those dark, depress-ing winter evenings in our Kedleston Road flat, sitting as close to the coal fire as I could; I would see the image of Mihir-*da*'s face.

But Mihir-*da*'s favourite stories were about Frank Worrall who had once come to dine at their house. I did not know who Frank Worrall was.

He was one of the 'Three Ws', he explained: Worrall, Everton Weekes and Clyde Walcott. They were in the West Indian team who toured England in the summer of 1950, and they had beaten England at Lord's.

Mihir-*da*'s eyes would light up in pleasure at the recollection, though he had not witnessed the match. That was a real milestone, he would say. For the first time ever the West Indians had shown England and Australia that the white man no longer ruled cricket. The Three Ws, all batsmen, were coloured, they were black men (Mihir-*da* said), and so were the spin bowlers Sonny Ramadhin and Alf Valentine. And though the West Indian team was still captained by a white person, John Goddard – Mihir-*da* said this with a scowl on his face – the tour was a triumph for the coloured players.

He taught me a calypso someone had composed after the West Indian victory at Lord's. It began

> *Cricket, lovely cricket*
> *At Lord's where I saw it,*
> *Yardley won the toss*
> *But Goddard won the test*

– and told the story of this victory. At the end of each stanza it had a catchy, jaunty refrain:

> *With those little pals of mine*
> *Ramadhin and Valentine*

In the years that followed I tried desperately but unsuccessfully to hear the actual song on the radio or buy the record. And so, I was only able to hear the calypso with my inner ear, in Mihir-*da*'s unmelodic voice, until much later, when I was sixteen or so, I found a copy of a recording in a music shop in south Calcutta.

I had grasped the significance of colour quite soon after we landed in England. A few months into our stay in the Warwick Road house in London, unhappy with our living arrangement, my parents began to go flat-hunting. One evening they returned, jubilant, having found a place they liked. They had put down a deposit. In the next few days, they were busy buying blankets, linen and the like. But then, when they went back to that house to leave some of our belongings there, the owner informed them that the flat was no longer available. There had been a mistake of some sort, it had already been rented out to someone else.

There was nothing my parents could do. I overheard them and my grandmother discuss the episode. That was when I first heard the words 'colour bar'.

At school – St Joseph's in Nottingham, Convent School in Derby – I was the only non-white student. My schoolmates did not know much about India or Indians – despite the fact that India had been, in the words of its most unloved viceroy, Lord Curzon, the 'Jewel in the Crown' of the British Empire. One or two of my classmates asked me about the 'Black Hole of Calcutta' (which I knew nothing of) – and when I asked my father he would reply angrily that that was all 'they' knew of Calcutta.

Some of my schoolmates thought I was a Red Indian, and they wanted to see my feathers. A young patient of my father's at the Derbyshire Royal Infirmary once asked to see his tomahawk –

which greatly mystified my father, for he had no idea what a tomahawk was. When I enlightened him, he was very indignant.

I would be amazed in those early years how ignorant they were about us, even my teachers, even the nuns. The first time my mother came to pick me up after school they had all gaped at her, children, teachers, parents alike. They wanted to know what she was wearing. They meant the sari. Was it a rope? Did she use it for the Indian rope trick?

At other times, someone at school would want to know whether tigers and elephants roamed the streets of Calcutta. Did we have tables and chairs? An older boy once asked me about 'Nero', and it took me some time to realize that he was speaking of Jawaharlal Nehru. My father and Mihir-*da* would react predictably to all this.

Still, neither the colour of my skin nor my Indiannness posed any serious problem for me. I was not traumatized by the occasional use of 'brownie' or 'sooty' or 'blackie' thrown at me in the playground or on the street or in the park. Even when, in a geography class at St Joseph's when Africa was our subject, several of my classmates looked pointedly in my direction when the word 'nigger' was used (whether by a teacher or a student I do not remember), I was not especially perturbed. I was more exasperated at their ignorance. In any case, most of the time they (and I) forgot that I was Indian, that I was brown-skinned, that I was not of their religion. Until Miss Sullivan entered my life some time in early 1954.

This was not the best of times. Derby County, relegated the previous year, was struggling in the Second Division. There seemed every chance of a slide into the Third Division. I had come to support a once-glorious side that was palpably a loser! Even Blackpool, in the First Division, could give me little comfort; they too had lost their winning ways, as we started the New Year.

By then I had discovered the *Football Special* – the green-coloured evening edition the *Derby Evening Telegraph* issued each Saturday evening, devoted entirely to that afternoon's football games. I had often wondered why, whenever I came to Dean's Newsagents on a Saturday evening, there was a small crowd of people, mostly men, a few boys, sometimes a woman or two, waiting inside the tiny store, or standing in the cold outside, smoking. I would come to purchase a packet of Maltesers or an Aero bar and had never paused to find out the reason for the crowd – till I was enlightened by someone, perhaps Harold Heldrich from next door, or the butcher's son, Tony Scatter-good, from across the road, or Graham, whose uncle the shop belonged to.

So a new ritual was established on Saturdays. I, too, joined the 'regulars' who waited for the *Special* at Dean's. I would reach the shop earlier than I needed to, eager to listen to the gossip, mostly about the Rams and its misfortunes, but occasionally other teams would be mentioned. My heart would be thudding as I walked back home clutching the newspaper, wondering how Blackpool had done, how Derby had done (if they were playing away).

Then came that Saturday when I looked disbelievingly at the FA Cup fifth-round results: Port Vale 2–Blackpool 0. The holders of the Cup had lost to a Third Division team. I stared in misery at the score line. Blackpool, Matthews, Mortensen – the whole crowd – was out of the Cup!

In the midst of all this I had to cope with Miss Sullivan. She had become our class teacher in mid-year because our previous teacher had left. And, for reasons I cannot remember or never knew, she disliked me from the very beginning. Her antipathy deepened into frank hostility when I refused to learn the cate-chism.

Till then, in all the time I had been in England, the Catholic
faith had never intruded in any problematic way upon my life. I
would quite mechanically say the Lord's Prayer and cross myself
and doff my school cap when passing a church. These rituals
posed no problem for me. At morning assembly I enjoyed singing
hymns just as I loved Christmas carols (as did my parents). Like
them, or perhaps because of them, my mother especially, I had
acquired an eclectic taste in music. I would listen to the *Rabindra-
sangeet* my mother sang, to Nat King Cole's 'A Blossom Fell' on
the radio, to Tex Ritter's song from *High Noon* on my gramophone, to hymns at morning prayer with equal pleasure. There
would be days when I would find myself replaying repeatedly,
inside my head, 'Onward, Christian Soldiers' or the soporific 'Jai
Jagadish Hare', an Indian devotional song, a *bhajan*, my mother
most often sang, softly, eyes closed, accompanied by the tinkle of
a pair of tiny cymbals in the morning, before breakfast, sitting
cross-legged in the bedroom corner that served as her prayer
area.

Away from school, especially at home, I was essentially
untouched by its religious commitments. Until Miss Sullivan
entered my life and demanded that we must learn the catechism
as a part of our regular schoolwork. By extension, it became part
of my homework. And I deeply resented this.

For those parents in India who sent their children to 'English
Medium' schools, this choice was a pragmatic one, for to be
taught in English, to know and speak English fluently, to understand English culture, gave their offspring an extra competitive
edge in life. These parents gave small thought to the religious
baggage that came with 'English Medium' instruction.

Perhaps this baggage was kept behind the scenes back in
India, since the pupils at the many branches of Loreto and St
Xavier's and their other brethren schools that dotted the Indian

townscapes were primarily non-Christians, mostly Hindus but also
Zoroastrians, Muslims and even some Jews. Perhaps the nuns and
priests who ran these institutions felt it prudent to keep the purely
religious aspect at a low profile. Certainly my mother could
not recollect ever having to learn or even read the catechism.

As for my father, Christianity – I doubt if he made any distinction between its denominations – was simply one region of
his cultural map. At some point in his life, in a wholly unselfcon-
scious way, he had come to admire the New Testament. And
above the headboard of my parents' bed hung not one but two
crucifixes. He explained to someone who asked about them that
he just liked to have them there, to look at them when he went to
bed, to see them when he rose in the morning. He also adored
Christmas carols and would sometimes cajole me, to my annoy-
ance, into singing his favourite ones, especially 'Silent Night', at
all odd times in the year, even in midsummer.

It was not so much the intrusion of the Catholic faith into my
home that troubled me but the catechism's talk of a god which
was 'their' God. I felt oppressed by its insistence on the One True
Church which was 'their' Church; and that outside this Church
there was no salvation. I resented this arrogance; after all, the celebrations of *Durga Puja* and *Kali Puja* were a part of the backdrop
of my earliest childhood in Calcutta. Without the least bit of reli-
giosity on my part, I resented the suggestion that only 'their' God
mattered.

Furthermore, there was all this talk in the catechism of sin and
guilt and punishment. As it was, my mother's constant exhorta-
tion had firmly entrenched into my mind certain ethical precepts:
the distinction between *nyay* and *anyay*, right and wrong; she had
drilled into me enough of the categories of oughts and ought-
nots. In my diary, which I started keeping from my ninth year, I
had to record, on a weekly basis, whether I had been 'good',

'obedient', 'kind' and such like. But at no point did my mother insist that these were 'Hindu values' or any religious values whatsoever. The precepts were of a soundly secular, temporal sort. Such notions as sin and guilt and Hell were firmly outside my ethical landscape.

For these reasons, the catechism was an unwelcome intrusion. Every time I dipped into its pages and was confronted with talk of sin, guilt, punishment and Hell, I felt a surge of terror.

I had known this kind of terror only once before – in Nottingham. I had gone with my parents to see a movie in which scientists had thawed out a prehistoric being, half-man, half-ape, that had lain buried under ice for a million years or more, somewhere in the Arctic. As this ape-man returned from limbo, watched fascinatedly by the movie scientists, he stirred slowly back to life, moving first his limbs and his head; then he opened his eyes; he gazed at the scientists, at us in the dark cinema. My father bent down and whispered in my ear that wasn't it amazing, those same eyes saw the world a million years ago.

I had no idea how long a million years was; but when I heard my father's words, I gazed back at those eyes and I was seized with the most awful sense of terror. I wanted to rise from my seat and run from the darkness out into the sunlight. That night, I could not sleep for many hours; I had to follow my father's advice and desperately thought of the images of Durga and Kali and Saraswati in the prayer room of our house in Calcutta.

I felt this same sort of terror when reading the catechism: the same blind impulse to free myself from its oppressive air and escape into daylight and sunshine and real life.

Of course I could never satisfy Miss Sullivan that I had learned the text, since I hadn't. I was often punished. One day, in view of the rest of my classmates, she made me kneel on the cold stone floor in one corner – to work on the catechism, as she said.

My schoolwork suffered badly. My parents met Miss Sullivan; they must have met the principal of Convent School. If they did it was to no avail. They speculated as to Miss Sullivan's motive. Mihir-*da* had no doubt. It was a matter of race, he would say darkly, his stammer becoming more pronounced.

6

Cup Final Day

Cup Final day! The very thought spread like a beautiful, comfortable warmth through the pores of my being as I woke that Saturday morning. It was May Day. I would be witnessing my first Cup Final – on television, of course – at the Heldriches' house next door, for my parents did not own one, despite my pleas. My mother refused to have one. She claimed it 'kills all social life'. She dreaded with all her gregarious soul the possibility that she might pay an evening visit to one of her growing band of English friends only to find that friend glued to the television, and she would have no choice but sit and watch along with her. She did not dislike watching television programmes – indeed, she would often go downstairs to the Amoses' when *What's My Line?* was showing. But one must not avoid socializing or entertaining; one must not allow the schedule of television programmes to control one's social life, she would say.

And so, I had to depend on the hospitality of others for my TV viewing: sometimes downstairs at the Amoses'; sometimes I would walk the few yards to Wheeldon Avenue to Graham Dean's house. But most times, I went next door. Come four o'clock on weekday evenings, I would ensconce myself in the bosom of the Heldrich family in their front living room. My friend was Harold, three or so years my senior, but there were Harold's younger sisters, Avis, about my age, and Janice, slightly younger.

Janice had large, luminous eyes and once in all innocence I had described them to my parents as eyes that looked like two moons. They had been greatly amused by what they took to be the first signs of my interest in girls, and this description was quickly relayed back to relatives in Calcutta – as I would discover to my astonishment several years later. Then there were Harold's older siblings, they were adults or almost adults – Barbara and Anne, two very pretty, young women, both working, both to be seen with boyfriends, and Terry, who played rugby.

Mrs Heldrich, their mother, was always very kind to me but I was rather afraid of Mr Heldrich: he was an aloof, taciturn man who scarcely seemed to notice my presence. He owned a furniture removal service of some kind, and there would always be a large van parked in front of their house. He was also one of our few neighbours who owned a car. At one time, he drove a Fiat. An Italian car was a rare thing to behold amid the Austins, Vauxhalls, Morrises and Fords, all stalwart English makes, and I would gaze at the Fiat in fascination.

My first Cup Final! I had recovered from the humiliation of Blackpool's demise in the fifth round, and had gained some pleasure in their League performance, for they recovered their form and finished high in the First Division. As for Derby County, they had ended perilously close to the relegation end of the Second Division but had somehow survived, and we heaved a gigantic, collective sigh of relief.

But this was to be Tom Finney's day, so the newspapers said, as surely as the previous year it had been Stanley Matthews's day.

The press took great satisfaction in what they saw was a pleasing symmetry. I learned the phrase 'History repeats itself': they were all sanguine that history would repeat itself, that Tom Finney would win his first Cup Final winner's medal as Matthews had done the year before.

My feelings towards Tom Finney were deeply ambivalent. Deep in my soul I admired him immensely, but I would feel a massive burden of guilt whenever I publicly admitted this. I felt I was being disloyal to Matthews. On one hand I had thrilled to the few glimpses I had had of Finney in full flight on television and newsreel clips. On the other hand I was jealous that he could play so adeptly on both wings while Matthews was always an outside right. I begrudged his ability to both make and score goals, and wished in exasperation that Matthews would score more often. I could not but help admire his bursts of speed down the wings. Overall, he was always a threat to Matthews – to Matthews's selection on the England team, to Matthews's reputation as the supreme football artiste.

My idea of heaven was an England forward line with Matthews on the right wing and Finney on the left, with Stanley Mortensen filling one of the inside forward positions. In fact, as my historical knowledge of English football grew I discovered that there had indeed been once when my heavenly ideal had been realized – an England team with a forward line of Matthews, Mortensen, Lawton, Mannion, Finney had demolished Portugal 10–0 in Lisbon in 1947. It was Mortensen's debut for England and he had celebrated this with four goals. I had already memorized the description of one of those goals and could see it in my mind's eye: Matthews from somewhere near the centre line making a long pass to Mortensen dashing down the right, Mortensen latching onto the ball, reaching almost the goal line and then, instead of passing the ball to Lawton in the centre as they all expected, he hit it from an 'impossible' angle and found the back of the net.

But this day I was prepared to be magnanimous. I, too, like the journalists, was in the mood for romance, wishing for the fairy-tale ending with Finney living happily ever after. I, too, willed him to a Cup triumph. I was prepared to give Graham, whose idol Finney was, his day of satisfaction.

There was something else about this day that gripped my imagination. It is surprising how little we actually saw our foot-balling heroes in action. Cricket was kindlier in this respect – since all the English test players played for County clubs, and there was only one major County Championship, we were assured of seeing in action the likes of Hutton and Compton and Typhoon Tyson and Fiery Freddie Truman at least once a summer – in our case in Derby or Chesterfield or Buxton where Derbyshire played its home matches. Even the visiting overseas teams came to play one's local County team. Furthermore, the test matches would all be televised.

Football was another matter: if one's local team was not in the top division, to watch a Billy Wright or Tom Finney or John Charles was the rarest of privileges; and we had to do some seri-ous travelling. To witness a foreign visiting team we had to go all the way to London. Television was not allowed to show the League or Cup matches; they would be permitted to beam only the occasional internationals – and sometimes, only the second halves. Even radio broadcasts were confined to second halves.

And so, in the absence of actual sightings of these men, I built my own images of them. I read about them in football books and newspapers; I studied intently their photographs; certain adjec-tives and phrases that seemed to be employed by all writers came to be intimately entwined with their names, and indeed I expanded my vocabulary from such readings: Jimmy Dickinson

was the 'thoughtful' halfback; Alf Ramsey was the 'cultured' fullback; Billy Wright was 'dependable' and 'consistent'; Trevor Ford
was the epitome of the 'courageous', 'bustling' centre forward;
John Charles was the 'complete' player; Wilf Mannion was 'elegant'; Len Shackleton was the 'clown prince' of soccer, and
Stanley Mortensen 'fast as a whippet'; Stanley Matthews could
'make a ball sit up and beg'.

The reason why the FA Cup Final had this extra aura lay in
part because it was one of the few football matches one could see
in its entirety on television.

But there were hours to spin before the start of the match.
Looking out through the living room window onto Kedleston
Road, it seemed to me that no one cared that it was Cup Final
day. The trolley buses hummed smoothly by as usual, their parallel poles making mysterious clicking sounds as they moved along
the overhead wires. The buses would carry their passengers into
town and disgorge them at Market Square. The people would
disperse. Some would make their way into Marks & Spencer,
Woolworths or Barlow & Taylor, others to the market inside
Guildhall, where the women would buy fruit and vegetables,
the children cheap toys and comic books. The older boys and
girls, who were already working, with Friday pay packets in
wallets and purses would walk up Friar Gate to Dixons the
record shop to listen, huddled together in soundproof booths,
to the latest imports from America – Frank Sinatra, Dean Martin,
Kitty Kallen, Nat King Cole or, nearer home, to Ruby Murray
or Joan Regan.

On any other Saturday I, too, would be on one of those
buses – with Graham perhaps, or Harold. On any other Saturday
I would be browsing in the magazine stall just inside the entrance
of Guildhall to see whether the latest *Charles Buchan's Football
Monthly* had arrived; or I would have paid a visit to the stamp

shop; or to the public library on Wardwick, to take out an Arthur Ransome *Swallows and Amazons* story. We would have revelled amid the Saturday morning throng on St Peter Street.

And after lunch, if there was no Rams game at the Baseball Ground, there was always the local West End team at the Rec; or the prospect of a very long walk that Harold and I often enjoyed sometimes accompanied by one or other of his younger sisters – a walk that might take us along Kedleston Road right out of Derby itself into one of its outlying suburbs.

Our parents scarcely knew of these sojourns; they did not worry one wit; they did not need to worry unless we returned unduly late. I was still not ten years old!

But not this Saturday. Instead, I stood by the window willing the hours to be gobbled up. Across the road, in front of a row of shops – which included Scattergood's, the butcher, whose daughter Susan, a few years older than me, had patiently and enthusiastically taught me to ride a bicycle – the pavement widened into a kind of small piazza. People, mostly women, to and from Scattergood's, or Buxton's the baker, or the greengrocer's shop which doubled as a post office, would pause to exchange greetings and share gossip. This day was no different, I noticed, and I felt deflated. Didn't they know this was Cup Final day?

From the living room, I must have heard the usual Saturday-morning noise coming from the adjoining kitchen: the sound of breakfast-making – the light slam of drawers being shut, the clink of cutlery, the flip-flop of my mother's bedroom slippers. As always she would be singing. Sometimes it would be a *Rabindra-sangeet* – and depending on the weather, this might be one of Tagore's many slow, contemplative *raga*-based pieces composed for the rainy season, or a joyous song celebrating spring; or I might hear a Hindi film song; or it might be 'Que Sera Sera', and

when she sang this, her Bengali, classically trained voice would go
to its highest note on the refrain.

On Saturdays, there was not the usual urgency to hurry
through breakfast; there would be no porridge which I loathed
but was forced to eat (because, my mother insisted, it would keep
me warm and make me grow) and no omelette and toast. On
Saturdays, from the living room, I would hear the low, rhythmic
gasp of a rolling pin as she made *luchi*, a circular, pancake-like
bread, a great favourite of mine which I would eat with a mod-
erately spiced potato curry. Sometimes, when I had consumed all
the curry I would eat a few extra luchi with sugar: I would pour
sugar onto a flat surface, then roll it so as to encase the sugar in
a kind of open-ended cylinder, and bite into it from one end,
taking care that the grains did not slither out of the other.

It was a very Bengali breakfast, like the ones we would have on
Sundays in our joint family home in Calcutta – my father, my
father's brothers, and we cousins, all together, sitting cross-
legged, yoga-style, on little wooden mats called *piris*, small rectangular platforms really, along the periphery of our dining
room. (Dining room is probably too grand a term: it was simply
a room where we ate.)

The adult womenfolk, my mother and her sisters-in-law, the
jas, my aunts, the wives of my uncles – the loose ends of their
saris, the *aachals*, pulled over their heads in deference to the presence of the older menfolk, squatted on their haunches in the
centre of the room, and served hot, soft, puffed-swollen *luchi* and
spiced vegetable curry, sometimes made from potato, sometimes
from aubergine.

The women would have their breakfast after their menfolk and
children had eaten and vacated the room. They would serve
themselves, save for a maid who might pour water into their
glasses. They would sit on the *piris* close together, in a small circle

with the food in dishes in the centre within everyone's reach; stooping over their *thali*, the traditional Indian brass utensil used as a plate, they would help themselves to the curry, by now cold, and *luchi* that had become flat and brittle and crusty as they always do when not served piping hot. These were the times when they set aside their differences and their mutually inflicted grievances. All the animosities and envy that emanated from the inequalities in their respective economic conditions, their respective husbands' and offspring's accomplishments, the differences in their successes and failures, all the resentments that would spill out at night into their husbands' weary ears in the privacy of their bedrooms, sometimes overheard by their children who they thought were fast asleep – all that would be suspended. These were the times for incessant, infinite, amiable, conspiratorial chatter; gossip about others not present, sometimes neighbours but mostly relatives – relatives they had all inherited when they married into our family.

So they would linger, licking dried-up, encrusted fingers, scraping the last particles of curry stuck to the *thalis*. The maid would wait patiently, resignedly.

In Derby, there were no *jas*, no comfortable, womanly, family chatter; only me to have breakfast with, a son who most often would be preoccupied with thoughts of other things. Yet she must have taken comfort in the way I relished my Saturday morning Bengali breakfast of *luchi* and curry and sugar.

History did not repeat itself. History does not usually repeat itself. Most events in history are unique. Historians have told us so. Now I know this well, but then I did not. Nor, apparently, did the journalists, for all their sagacity – or perhaps beneath their hardbitten, pragmatic veneers were cores of sentimentality which on Cup Final day, the most ancient of sporting events, filled with lore and magic, they could not quite suppress.

This event in history was quite unique. The circumstances that constituted the Cup Final in May 1954 were nothing like the circumstances that constituted the Cup Final in May 1953. Then Matthews rose to the occasion, as did Mortensen, as did Johnston, as did 'little' Ernie Taylor, as did left winger Bill Perry. This time, Finney could not deliver.

In the darkened living room at the Heldriches, I sat enthralled, absorbing sights and sounds that I had only read about, that I could only imagine before: a hundred thousand voices singing an immensely sentimental song, 'Over the Mountain, Over the Sea'; the royal box where the Queen Mother sat; the teams, Preston North End and West Bromwich Albion, emerging from the shadows of the tunnel led by captains Tom Finney and Len Millard; the rattles; the rosettes; the songsheets waved in unison like so many pennants; the presentation of the teams to royalty; the nervous tension in the faces of the players.

In the course of my self-education in football, I had encountered the word tradition various times – as 'Wembley tradition', 'Cup Final tradition'. It was only that May Day, however, that I felt, however tremulously, the idea of tradition.

And yet this still, only through television. I was still seeing a flat image, not the real thing. I was still only an observer, not participant; I was not in the scene, nor of it, in the sense I was of the scene, was part of it when inside the Baseball Ground. We were even deprived of the colour of it all – the images which I so greedily imbibed were in black and grey and white. There remained within me that faint sense of inadequacy, that I was still missing something of this tradition.

Finney had, as one reporter described the next day, a footballer's nightmare. We grieved with him and for him as the fortunes of the two teams waxed and waned. In the end Preston lost by the odd goal of five. What had begun in everyone's mind (except the West Bromwich fans) as the Finney Final ended as Finney's Failure.

I should have learned a lesson that day – not only about history but that football, like life itself, is full of surprises, replete with disappointments. But then, to be a lover of the game, whether as player or fan or journalist, is to be an immense optimist, a romantic of the highest order – for how else can one support a team?

How else could I look on with hope and expectation as, a few weeks later, England went to Hungary in search of revenge for what had happened in Wembley six months previously? How else could I restore my faith when Hungary once more slaughtered England, seven goals to one, in the worst ever defeat of an English team? That neither Matthews nor Mortensen (whose match against Hungary at Wembley, it turned out, was his last international) was playing was no consolation. How else except for being a profound optimist, harbouring enormous faith, could anyone go on hoping when the World Cup began in Switzerland in June?

By now I knew my World Cup history. I was painfully aware of what had happened to England in 1950. For the first time that year, England had 'condescended' (a new word) to compete in the World Cup. Before then, they had 'disdained' (another new word) from entering the competition. I could not follow the arguments for this, except that some felt that England had invented football, they had given it to the world, they had taught others how it should be played – and what could the world teach the teacher? They had played other countries at home and abroad before and after the war, had never lost on their own soil to a foreign team, and even abroad they had done, mostly, very well. So what could they gain by playing in the World Cup? They had nothing to prove.

So when they decided, finally, to enter the World Cup

competition in Brazil in 1950, they went in full confidence of their self-worth. Besides, my books said, they were counted as one of the two favourites (along with Brazil) to win the Cup.

Then they lost to the United States of America! Reading about this match I felt desolate, humiliated. There was one picture that appeared repeatedly in the articles I read on this game: Bert Williams, the England and Wolves goalkeeper (whom I had adopted as my favourite goalkeeper – because he was supposed to be the best goalkeeper in England at that time, because he was called 'The Cat' on account of his agility, because he looked wonderful in his polo-neck jersey, because there was something mysterious in his face), looking on helplessly and in dismay as the ball eludes him and America scores the all-important winning goal. Every time I looked at this picture, I squirmed in embarrassment.

Would that kind of thing happen again? Mercifully, it did not. Eventually, England reached the quarter-finals and lost to Uruguay in a game I watched on television sitting on my usual pouffe in the Amoses' living room, a match they could well have won but for the goalkeeper Gil Merrick's blunders – the same Merrick who had let through thirteen Hungarian goals that past year.

I was a bit afraid of the South Americans – ever since I read that the stupendous Rio de Janeiro stadium had a moat surrounding the pitch to prevent irate, enraged spectators from attacking referees, linesmen and opposition players. This apprehension was compounded by awe when I had my first glimpse of these footballers from Uruguay and Brazil. Their footwork and skill made the Scottish – who were trounced seven goals to nil in one match by Uruguay, and Graham's favourite Scottish goalkeeper, Martin, was the primary object of the newspaper's ridicule – and English players I had so far seen (Matthews and

Finney excepted, of course!) seem like clumsy oafs. But there was still Hungary – out-and-out favourites to win the World Cup, everyone said in the papers – and I not only believed them, once England lost to Uruguay, I wanted Hungary to win. By now, the Hungarians – Gyula Grosics and Ferenc Puskás and Nándor Hidegkuti and Zoltán Czibor and Sándor Kocsis – were like old friends! I could identify with the Hungarians in a way I could not with the Brazilians and the Uruguayans, the finalists in 1950.

Football is full of surprises and disappointments – a lesson I learned and remembered. Leading up to the final stages Hungary chalked up scores that were more like points in a rugby game: Hungary 10–Luxembourg 0, Hungary 9–South Korea 0, Hungary 8–Germany 3. And then, after beating Brazil in the quarter-final in what the English reporters gleefully (this kind of happening could not occur in England, they wrote complacently) dubbed the 'Battle of Berne' – 'battle' meant not in the metaphorical sense of an epic, heroic struggle, but literally, both on the pitch and in the dressing room afterwards – and then Uruguay in the semi-final, we could only wait to savour their deserved victory in the World Cup final against Germany. I, too, willed Puskás and company to victory as I had willed Tom Finney.

Life and football are rife with disappointment. Once more. I watched in unbelieving dismay as Hungary lost a 2–0 lead and, ultimately, the match itself by three goals to two.

New names entered my footballing knowledge base: Juan Schiaffino of Uruguay, Didi of Brazil, Fritz Walter of Germany, Ernst Ocwirk of Austria. The World Cup of 1954 was, in a proper sense, my international debut!

7

Tangerine Week

That autumn was suffused with the oddest mixture of ecstasy and sadness. The ecstasy definitely dominated, it was sharply delineated, unequivocal, like buckets of vivid colour, tangerine to be precise, splashed on a white wall. The sadness, which came later, was more an ache, muted, indefinable, fuzzy-edged.

Early in September, just after the end of the cricket season and the beginning of the new football season, my parents and I went to Blackpool for a week. This was our first family vacation since a holiday in Darjeeling when I was four or five. I remember nothing of that time, but there were pictures of me riding a pony, of my mother sitting side saddle on a horse.

My father suggested 'a real English holiday at the seaside'. There was only one place to go as far as I was concerned – Blackpool.

We went by coach. I had never before taken such a long road journey, in fact I had hardly ever travelled by road anywhere, and was soon complaining of nausea; somehow I managed to hold back till we stopped in Manchester for lunch, where, at the coach station, I vomited long and violently on the side of the road while passengers and passers-by watched and commiserated. I learned a new term: 'road sickness'.

In Blackpool, almost as soon as we had unpacked our bags in our small, family-run hotel, I dragged my father to Bloomfield Road, the home of Blackpool Football Club. It was a weekday, there was no prospect of a match that day, but still I hoped to catch sight of Matthews and Mortensen and perhaps get their autographs. That afternoon, we reached it too late. The place was deserted, the gates locked. A gatesman told us that training was over for the day; he suggested that we come back the next morning.

Which we did. And this time I was lucky, luckier than I could have ever hoped. Later that evening, back in the hotel, as my parents freshened up for dinner, I gleefully scrawled an entry in my diary: 'I met S. Matthews and S. Mortensen and took photographs with them.' I doubt if I paid any attention to the food that evening or to the other guests. I could only replay in my head those brief, dazzling, dizzying, tremulous minutes when I first caught sight of Stanley Mortensen, as dapper in real life as in the pictures, immaculately suited; and then minutes later, Stanley Matthews driving into the parking area, alighting, and walking crisply towards where we stood near the surprisingly deserted Players' Entrance area.

They both signed my autograph book, and obliged when my father asked whether he could take their photographs with me, each separately. Mortensen said something to me cheerfully, with a grin on his face – afterwards I could not remember what he said. Matthews was more serious but not unfriendly, and posed with his arm resting lightly around my shoulders, and as we stood for the picture he asked me in a slightly gruff voice, 'What's your name, son?' I suppose I must have said, not 'Subrata' but 'Poupeé'. Other players straggled in by and by – Ernie Taylor, smaller than my father, the lanky Harry Johnston, the sallow-skinned Bill Perry, and very quickly my brand new autograph book was filled with the signatures of almost the whole Cup winning team.

But that evening, though we went to the top of Blackpool Tower, what remained was the ecstasy of that moment, the images of the handsome 'Morty' and of a dark-grey suited, speckled-tied, calm face with the faintest hint of a smile, a receding hairline just like my father's in my parents' wedding picture, the light pressure of an arm around my shoulder, and the sound of a low, serious voice asking my name.

The day after, a Saturday, the Blackpool first team was playing away, but I still insisted that we should go to the ground and watch the reserve team play. I wanted to see with my own eyes the tangerine colour of the Blackpool jersey – its exact colour. My mother probably spent the afternoon exploring the shops, writing postcards to friends in Derby and Nottingham, and perhaps to my grandmother and uncle back in Calcutta. I really did not particularly care. I went with my father and a man named Mr Kirkus to Bloomfield Road. He was a fellow guest at the hotel whom I had quickly befriended when I learned that he, too, was a Blackpool supporter. My luck still held, for Mortensen was playing that afternoon in the reserve team. The match was surprisingly well attended considering that it was a reserve team match, and I was deflated somewhat when Blackpool lost to Liverpool by five goals to two. It was enlivened only by the sight of Mortensen making the kind of dash down the middle in pursuit of the ball that I had read about and memorized. I can no longer remember whether he scored any goals.

The rest of that holiday week was something of an anticlimax, of course. My father's appetite for circuses and zoos was prodigious, and when he learned that there was a circus performing nearby, we had to go. His cup of happiness brimmed over when

Stanley Matthews and me, Blackpool, 1954.

we saw a Royal Bengal tiger in a kind of enclosed zoo. He could spend hours gazing at tigers. One of the first excursions we made when we first arrived in London was a visit to the Regent's Park Zoo. Returning home, he had immediately set about painting in watercolours a Royal Bengal tiger we had seen there.

I tasted my first sea water and hated it. I spluttered and flailed my arms and legs like a helpless frog, trying to learn to swim while my father stood in the water and propped up my stomach from below, so that I lay horizontally. The brine engulfed me, my nostrils, my mouth, my ears, my eyes; its pungency took me by surprise. I felt very foolish, because every boy and girl around me, every man and woman, could swim and I could not. I became more conscious than I had ever been in England of my brownness amidst all the pink and white.

My discomfort was compounded by the sight of my mother who looked quite out of place in her sari, sitting placidly amidst the teeming masses of half-naked bodies on the beach. Before we set off from Derby, my father had tried to convince her to wear a swimsuit; he had even stopped at Marks & Spencer on his way home from the Royal Infirmary intending to buy one. But he knew my mother – she was a stubborn person, and no amount of cajoling on his part would have made her change her mind on this matter. I heard her tell my father that she had never worn anything but a sari since leaving school at sixteen. She had even disregarded his suggestion that she should wear slacks to ward off the cold. And so, there she would sit on the Blackpool beach, quite unperturbed, rising occasionally, going to the edge, where she would pull up the hem of the sari to above her shin, and wade into the shallow water and enjoy the sensation of it lapping round her ankles.

I overheard her remind my father of the last time they had been to the seaside. It had been just after their marriage, and the whole of the joint family had gone to Puri, a resort in Orissa, an adjacent state to Bengal. There, while the menfolk and the older children swam and splashed around, she and my aunts – her *jas* – had stood at the water's edge in exactly the same way.

Frankly, once I had had my days at Bloomfield Road, and had visited Stanley Mortensen's sports shop (he was not there that day, however), my interest in Blackpool waned sharply. I think my parents enjoyed themselves more than I did. They both revelled being in the midst of crowds, especially in the evenings when we would be strolling along the sea front when it looked as if the whole city was out walking. The air was filled with music blaring from radios and gramophones, and I must have heard Frank Sinatra's lazy voice singing 'Three Coins in the Fountain' a hundred times in those seven days. It was a place for lovers: I had never seen so many in the space of such a short time and in such density as I did in Blackpool that week – and I would gaze furtively at couples in passionate embraces, some while walking, some standing perfectly still, some sitting on benches, and some lying on top of each other on the sand. That week, perhaps for the first time, I felt the presence of sex all around me.

The long summer had dulled my memory of the unpleasant experiences of the previous term in Convent School. No doubt my parents had thought it had been just one of those unfortunate but temporary things that one gets caught up in inexplicably, and that it was now behind us.

It took just a few weeks for me to realize that it had not been a nightmare after all. Miss Sullivan was still my class teacher and the summer had not mellowed her. At my tearful insistence, my parents decided to take me out of Convent School. By now I had several other friends in the neighbourhood who had either attended or still went to Ashgate Primary School, about a mile-and-a-half walk away from Kedleston Road. Neighbours whom my parents consulted recommended this school. It was not fancy by any means, they warned my parents, but they had a good record in the 11-plus.

Thus reassured, there followed an interview with the headmaster of Ashgate. And so, one dark, wet, depressing November day, a month or so after my tenth birthday, I sadly said goodbye to my Convent School friends. The next day I wrote in my diary: 'I have started a new school today. It's called Ashgate.'

8

Goalkeeper for a Friend

Ashgate School, on Ashbourne Road, was housed in a bulky, brooding structure built most likely in the first quarter of the twentieth century to which smaller, more recent and architecturally more unprepossessing buildings had been added at the back, away from the main road. The scene as a whole was faintly menacing. The one redeeming feature, I noticed immediately that first day, was an ample playground in the front and the two sides, a kind of release after the tiny, claustrophobic patch of cement in Convent School that we had had to make do with. The students were not required to wear school uniforms, and though one could buy, in one of the shops in town that specialized in schoolwear, blazers and scarves and caps in Ashgate's grass-green and canary-yellow colours, very few did, for few could afford to. And so, except for the odd boy or girl here and there, sporting a school cap or scarf or, rarer still, a school blazer, the clothes they wore to school were mostly in colours that deftly concealed dirt and the need to wash. It was almost as if the collective intent was to meld into the very texture of the physical surroundings; on dark, sullen, rain-drenched, windswept days, it would seem they were all, indeed, one: sky, school, ground and students.

Ashgate had both boys and girls as students but it was not co-educational in the way I was familiar with at St Joseph's and Convent School: we did not take classes together, nor were we allowed to mingle during schooltime. The girls' section was in the front part of the main building; the boys' classrooms were at the back of the main building and in a large building at the back. So far as I recall, we had our headmaster and they had their headmistress. During free time, there was a small part of the boys' and the girls' sections of the playground that intersected, but by and large, the twain never met. Nor, at that time, were we particularly interested in girls.

I did not know quite what to expect from Ashgate. In the almost cloistered world of Convent School, I had heard, vaguely, stories that had stoked my apprehension when the time came for me to go to my new school. I heard that there were boys who used swear words in the hearing of their teachers; that after school hours there were fisticuff fights on its playground; that some boys were so uncontrollable they had to be dispatched to Borstal.

These rumours about a free, municipal school relayed with relish in the fee-paying environs of Convent School, were largely apocryphal; yet like all rumours they contained a smattering of truth. While the majority of the boys were, as boys go, disciplined and anxious to avoid trouble, the school had its share of the oddball, the misfit, the rebel, the bully and the outright delinquent. There were those sullen, glowering boys with hostile glints in their eyes ever ready to pick a quarrel or start a fight, scarcely batting an eyelid when their form teachers punished them with lashes of the cane on outstretched palms or plimsoles on their behinds.

Fights – systematic fist fights – contrary to the stories I had heard, were not commonplace, but they were not that infrequent either. They were usually staged in some corner of the school grounds, in a convenient nook tucked well out of sight of the teachers' wary eyes. They were mostly held – arranged – after school hours, after all the teachers and most of the boys had gone. Those who remained were the fighters themselves and their cronies and supporters.

There was a slightly theatrical, ritualistic air to these proceedings. They seldom began impetuously. Rather, they would originate in some vague disagreement or a deliberate provocation – a taunt, a jeer, a challenge, a verbal throwing of the gauntlet which the opponent had little choice but to accept. But the fight would usually be saved for later. And as the word spread, a few would wait with keen anticipation for the four o'clock bell to ring and then, impatiently, for the school to disperse, the teachers to depart on their bicycles or motorbikes or, in one or two cases, battered, out-of-date cars, till the playground was deserted and still.

I came to know this ritual well, because my best friend in Ashgate was one of the two or three in the whole school who was involved in several fights in my two years at Ashgate. His name was David Newman.

It took all of one day and a few probes for each of us to recognize a kindred soul in the other: that we both lived and breathed football. On the first day of our encounter, we tested each other aggressively with certain acid tests of footballing knowledge. Then, satisfied with what the other knew, and having agreed on several important points – the best English goalkeeper of the time (Bert Williams of Wolves), the worst goalkeeper (Gil Merrick of Birmingham), the best all-round player (John Charles of Leeds United), the best Scottish forward (Billy Liddell of

Liverpool) – we were willing to disagree amicably on the fundamental matter: for me, of course, Matthews was the supreme
artist, the *Maestro*, the greatest winger ever seen; David insisted
that Tom Finney was the far better player – and gave the usual
reasons that had always troubled me, because they were unan-
swerable: he could play on both wings and as a centre forward, he
could both create and score goals, he was, simply, more versatile
(another word I learned from the journalists). I would shrug my
shoulders. Matthews was Matthews! Everyone knew him, all over
the world, even those who had no interest in football would flock
to see him play – just because 'he was there' – just as people who
had no interest in cricket would go to see Sir Donald Bradman.
He was – and here I would use the phrase I had picked up from
the newspapers – a 'household name'.

My mother laughed when she saw us together the first time.
We must have made an odd pair. Physically, I could not escape my
Bengali genes; I was smaller than the average English boy of my
age, almost skinny, not very strong, with spindly legs and knob-
bly knees that, for some reason, were perpetually grey as if
covered with grime, and a slightly beaky nose. David was taller
than most of the boys in our class, loose-limbed and muscular.
Already he had a strong physical presence. He was also inherently
rebellious in nature, a contrast to my general timidity, and this
rebellious streak would surface every now and then in different
ways as, for example, in the way he kept his hair swept back in the
manner of the Teddy boys we would see on the streets.

Football was David's primary passion, but fighting came a
close second. He was, physically and psychologically, a fighter –
not interested in brawling or wrestling in the uncouth manner
that boys indulge in on the playground at times of disagreement,
but real fist fighting, the way men once fought in rude rings
before boxing gloves were introduced. David was not naturally

quarrelsome nor a bully. He just liked to fight. He never picked a fight. But given half a chance, the hint of a challenge, his eyes would glitter. He rejoiced in the prospect of a fight whenever or wherever the chance arose.

Thus, there was an aura of toughness about him. This was enhanced by the fact that he was naturally good at sports. Within days of arriving at Ashgate, I learned that he was a good goal-keeper. Though we were in the third form, and there was a higher form, he had already laid claims as the school football team's reserve goalkeeper. That year, when the first team goalie John Hammond (whom we revered) could not play for some reason or other, David had his chance.

To have a goalkeeper for a friend! I could not have asked for more – my fascination with the very idea of the goalkeeper had not abated since those first encounters on the playing fields in Nottingham.

Later, when summer arrived, I found that he was just as tal-ented as a batsman in cricket.

In Ashgate, each form was split into three sections. In con-temporary jargon, we were 'streamed': the academically brightest were placed in the 'A' section, and the academically worst in the 'C' section. The 'B' section had those in between. And so when I was admitted to Ashgate, I was put in form 3A. David Newman was in my class.

We looked at the boys in 3C (and 4C) with some appre-hension. They were the tough ones, with a smattering of delinquent-like figures. The teachers of the 'C' classes were nec-essarily tougher than our teachers or those of the 'B' classes, and we were almost as apprehensive of them as we were of the boys. Once Mr Craig, the teacher of 3C, took over our class for arts and crafts – I do not recall when we were ever so meek, or so quiet!

Perhaps the most feared boy in the school was Graham Taylor

of 3C. He was a Jamaican, and seeing his brown complexion, I thought, at first, that he was from India. This was my first experience of another non-white boy in the same school as I was. Yet his hair was brown not black, and crinkly, and his features were not Indian. It was only when I noticed a certain resemblance between his features and the West Indian bowler Alf Valentine (of 'With those little pals of mine / Ramadhin and Valentine' fame), that I deduced he was from the West Indies.

Graham Taylor seemed to dwell perpetually in a private, dark, intense, brooding universe. I would sometimes see him sitting alone in some corner of the playground, motionless and moody at lunchtime or at afternoon break, glowering unseeingly at some distant object. What most frightened us – me at least – was his whimsical nature. We could never predict who or what would randomly raise his ire. He might stroll up to an unsuspecting boy, chosen quite arbitrarily, and taunt him. It seemed to me that his intent was to create a situation in which his hapless victim had no recourse but to accept his challenge to a fight – for the sake of pride or from fear of being branded a coward by others if he refused. There were times when he would not complete the kill. Perhaps his pleasure lay in the terror that would inexorably well up in his quarry at the prospect, the imminence of a fight later that day. Graham Taylor might just not show up. He was, I suppose, by nature a sadist. I know how his victims felt because I was one of them. He challenged me to a fight one morning and I spent the better part of that day sick with apprehension. Yet nothing transpired.

Perhaps the reason why I attracted Graham Taylor's attention was my friendship with David Newman, for David was the one boy who was not only not afraid of Taylor but was openly contemptuous towards him. They were unabashed enemies. I heard that they had fought once before I came to Ashgate, and in that first few months there was often the threat of a confrontation. Finally, one spring day, the two agreed to a fight.

Before that evening I had never seen two flesh-and-blood human beings engaged in a fist fight. At St Joseph's and even at Convent School, boys would occasionally engage in a free-for-all, but those would never last for long. The nuns were surprisingly indulgent, perhaps in deference to the 'boys will be boys' adage, but only up to a point.

When we lived in Calcutta, I would get glimpses of the aftermath of a fight, for one of my male cousins, three years older than me, would be perpetually embroiled in brawls with neighbourhood boys. Sitting or playing in the courtyard of our joint family house, we would suddenly hear shouts, loud voices – a higher noise level than was usual amid the closely packed neighbourhoods of the north side of the city, where one could ordinarily hear with no effort the crackle of a radio from the house next door, or neighbouring womenfolk scolding servants or haggling with obdurate door-to-door vendors, or a girl practising her musical scales from the house across the lane – then there would be more shouts closer by, and then the thud of bare feet running on the gravelly lane outside, and my cousin would enter the green wooden door leading into our courtyard, with blood running from his nose or an already swelling eye. The nose or the eye would be tended to swiftly, especially if my father was at home, but inevitably, my cousin's mother, perpetually frustrated by the scrapes he would get into on a daily basis, would slap him hard on the cheeks, once, twice or as many times as she could before one of her *jas* interceded, and my cousin would be sent packing upstairs to the room he shared with his siblings. Yet I had never witnessed the actual act by which my cousin's nose would be bloodied or his eyes would be slit. I could only imagine the event.

As for real boxing, with gloves, I had a vague remembrance,

soon after we arrived in England, of the excitement on the radio over a fight between Randolph Turpin, an English boxer, and the American Sugar Ray Robinson. And apart from a few radio broadcasts of boxing events, my only exposures to this sport which frankly did not really interest me (until another Englishman, Don Cockles, fought another American, Rocky Marciano) were occasional newsreel footages at the cinema.

Even those were mere images on the screen – abstractions, patterns of grey of varying intensity.

That evening, as David Newman and Graham Taylor took off their pullovers and then their shirts, I began to feel distinctly queasy. I could not stand still, not because of the cold but from nervous anticipation of something I had no experience of.

The fight began and so did the shouting. 'TWO-FOUR-SIX-EIGHT, WHOM DO WE APPRECIATE?' yelled the supporters. 'D-A-V-I-D,' shouted some; 'G-R-A-H-A-M,' responded the others.

I could only watch with fascinated and gathering horror. Every time one or the other's fist made contact with a chin or an eye or the chest, making a dreadful, muted thud, I would flinch. This was a fist fight, not a boxing match. There were no rounds, no referees, no seconds, no Marquess of Queensberry rules to abide by. Once begun it must continue to some inevitable conclusion. I was astonished by their capacity to absorb and mete out so much punishment. I could see that each was being damaged by the other's blows, by the fierce force of one set of white knuckles pounding the other's face. Yet they went on. They could not stop. They continued, minute after minute, silently save for the occasional grunt of effort or pain or both, and the thud of flesh meeting flesh.

The cronies' shouts gradually subsided, reduced to sporadic, uncertain, unconvincing yelps of encouragement. We were all, by now, rather palc.

Neither fighter would concede defeat; nor was one so superior that there was a prospect of a knockdown, let alone a knockout. As the fight continued, I was not sure for how long, we could see that both were exhausted, both panting heavily, with gashes and bruises and already swollen faces. I could see a cut above one of David's eyes, and a smear of blood.

Ultimately, someone's good sense prevailed; or perhaps we were getting bored with no prospect of a 'kill' in sight; or perhaps it was getting too cold to just stand around any longer. Whatever the reason, someone shouted peremptorily, startling the others, ordering the two to stop. The others joined in, in unison, in relief. Fists dropped in exhaustion. They both sank to the ground, their hair, faces and torsos bathed in sweat. They would fight another day, prompted by one flimsy reason or another, but for the time being honour had been saved for both.

We were total soulmates, David Newman and I, bound to each other by a passion and a commitment to football that no one else shared or could match in intensity. I wondered how I had survived without him before. Our universe was governed by the game. British geography, British history and even English Literature made sense to us only in footballing terms. When Mr Graham, our Form 3A teacher, read *Kidnapped* to us in the final hour of Friday afternoons, and we learned that Robert Louis Stevenson was born in Edinburgh, David and I exchanged knowing looks: Edinburgh was the home of the Heart of Midlothian ('Hearts') and Hibernian ('Hibs'), our respective favourite Scottish teams. When we read about the Roman settlement in Bath, and saw on the map that Bath was near Bristol, we thought of John Atyeo, the centre forward of Bristol Rovers. When London was mentioned, it was, of course, Arsenal and Tottenham and Chelsea that came to mind. When learning about the cotton mills of Lancashire, we could only think of

Manchester United and Manchester City, of Preston North End, of Blackburn Rovers; when the woollen mills of Yorkshire cropped up, our thoughts turned simultaneously to John Charles and Leeds United. And when Mr Graham spoke one time about prisoners-of-war, we at first drew a blank – until he used the abbreviation, 'POW' – when we thought immediately of Bert Trautmann, Manchester City's former POW, German goal-keeper. Even our mathematical judgements were warped by football: when Mr Graham taught us the concept of 'ratio', for several days I thought the word was 'horatio', perhaps in honour of Horatio 'Raich' Carter, Derby County's inside right in its glory days after the war.

The only history that really mattered to us was the history of football. We seeped ourselves in it. We secured, David and I, by the oddest means, old football annuals, from the 1940s. Sometimes, a boy would simply give us a book that had no meaning for them any more; sometimes we traded something or another; we collected 'football cards' – at one time they would come inside cigarette packets, but now were sold with packets of chewing gum and bubble gum which we bought from the little store across from the school on Ashbourne Road – and such were the sizes of our respective collections we could afford to exchange them for obsolete football books.

We pored over these old books. Players of the past, whom we would never see anywhere, on newsreel or on television, became as real to us, as much a part of our lives, as our current idols. We would talk about Derby County's fabulous FA Cup team of 1946 as if we knew the players personally – Raich Carter, and Peter Doherty, and Sammy Crooks and Duncan Daily and Jack Stamps, the captain.

I would study, in sorrow, descriptions and pictures of the 1948 FA Cup Final in which Manchester United beat Blackpool by four goals to two, while David took delight in reading how Wolves (with his beloved Bert Williams) had beaten Leicester City at Wembley the next year.

We reached further back: to Herbert Chapman and his great Arsenal of the 1930s, and Alex James; to Stevie Bloomer, the 'greatest centre forward of his time', who played for Derby and England before the First World War; to Dixie Dean of Everton who scored sixty League goals one season, a record that still stood; to Billy Meredith, a mysterious-looking Welshman who used to chew a toothpick on the field. To us, there was nothing remote about these men, nothing shadowy; never mind that some of them were dead. If I learned something about the nature of history from football, it was that there was a seamless continuity between past and present. The past was important because we could not make sense of the football of our time unless we knew what had happened before. Above all, I imbibed a sense of awe regarding tradition. Even the colours of the shirts the teams wore in our time were almost all rooted in the remote past. We gazed at old football cards of players from Aston Villa and Sunderland and Glasgow Celtic from the 1930s and 1920s – they wore the same strips that we would now see Peter McParland or Len Shackleton or Jock Stein wear. It was all of one coherent piece.

In December, we shared a magical fortnight, David and I. On 1 December, midweek, England defeated Germany at Wembley three goals to one. I watched the match that evening on the Amoses' television; I watched as Matthews turned on the kind of sorcery that I had only read of, that I could only imagine. Roy Bentley, Len Shackleton and Ronnie Allen scored the goals but the match was Matthews's and at last I knew why he was the *Maestro*. I went to bed with the music of his magic ringing in my head, I woke next morning and the music was still playing; that day, on the playground, it was all I could think of, talk of. David, perhaps jealous on Tom Finney's behalf, would have liked to change the subject, but for my sake he took the trouble to share in my ecstasy.

That evening, I realized that for some of the journalists and other adults, the game was not about Matthews. Scotland and England may have been 'auld enemies', but Germany was, since 1938, England's 'new enemy'; the football pundits had not forgotten that the England national team playing Germany in Berlin had been forced to give the Nazi salute. Furthermore, the end of the war in Europe was merely ten years old. People of that generation – they included my friends' fathers, such as Mr Dean, Graham's father – perceived the German team not so much as footballers but as Germans, as the soldiers they had fought against; the match as a continuation of the war. The pleasure they derived from England's victory in Wembley that afternoon was a continuation of the elation they had felt on VE Day.

Almost two weeks later, I sat in front of the Amoses' television set once more, this time to experience the novelty of a floodlit evening match between Wolverhampton Wanderers, the reigning League champions, and Honved of Hungary. We had talked of little else in school, David and I and a few of our other friends. The newspapers, too – for the great Puskás would be playing for Honved. No one was fooled that this was supposed to be a 'friendly': memories of the Hungarian two-time savaging of England were vivid in people's minds. Here was a glimmer of hope that that humiliation could be assuaged to some extent.

As in the German situation, there was an extra edge to this match that had nothing to do with football. I had heard the term 'Iron Curtain' the previous year, but had the haziest sense of its meaning. New words entered my vocabulary: 'communists' and 'communism'; 'democracy' and 'free world'. England's defeats last year were not simply to a foreign team, but to a team from the Iron Curtain countries, a team from a communist nation. And now, Honved, a club belonging to this communist nation, would be playing against a club that was part of a democratic nation. This was a battle between communism and the free world.

I watched enthralled as the ghostly images were made ghostlier still by the floodlights and fog; the free world won, England won, Wolves won. Two goals down at half-time, they rallied in the second half with two goals from Roy Swinbourne and a third from outside right Johnny Hancocks. The next day, the papers were ecstatic. Pleased though I was, even I felt uneasy at the extravagant claims made on Wolves' behalf: the greatest club in the world, the headlines roared. Graham Dean was all beams. So was David, for the sake of his hero Bert Williams, the Wolves goalkeeper.

In transferring me from Convent School to Ashgate, my parents may have thought that I had moved to a socially inferior milieu. My friends at Convent School came from middle-class backgrounds, like Graham Dean, whose father worked in an office of some sort. They came from the professions or what we now call white-collar occupations.

The boys I knew well in Ashgate were almost all from working-class families. David's father was a postman, another boy I came to know told me that his dad was a coalman, another's was a fitter in the Rolls-Royce plant. It was true that at least one boy who had gone to Ashgate before I joined, two years my senior, who lived a few houses down from us, with whom I came to be very friendly (his name was Robin Darbyshire) came from a solidly middle-class background. I believe his father was head of the English department at the local college of technology. Another Ashgate friend's father – they too lived on Kedleston

Road just across from the Darbyshires and this friend's name was Alan Potter – worked in a bank or a building society. But by and large, Ashgate was a school populated by working-class children.

For almost all of them, I was, I suppose, a new experience. I was probably the first Asian or African – the first boy 'of colour' – to enter into their homes. I was most likely the first 'foreigner' of any sort their parents had met.

Which is why it was remarkable how easily I was assimilated into this new culture. If I felt in no way different from the boys in Ashgate, then so too did they feel that I was one of them. The few times I was verbally abused along racial lines – called 'blackie' or 'darkie' or 'nigger' or some such word – they were outside the school, and the perpetrators were unknowns, some passing lout on a bicycle or a youth in the town's swimming pool. Such incidents did not affect me unduly.

The one genuinely unpleasant experience – unpleasant because it was prolonged – occurred for a period of over a month, perhaps two, on my daily morning walk to school.

There was no convenient bus route to Ashgate from Kedleston Road, and so, before I acquired my first bicycle on my eleventh birthday, I had to walk. It took just over twenty minutes, down Cowley Street, past the Rec, along Mackworth Road to Ashbourne Road, then cross over to the other side to the school gate.

I enjoyed these walks. I was never bored, for each day it posed a challenge. Sometimes I would take a small rubber ball and become Stanley Matthews and dribble it between and around imaginary opponents. The road to school then became one gigantically long, ribbon-like football field. Or, when accompanied by a friend, we would pass the ball to each other as we ran, an exhibition in the art of passing; we became Tom Finney and Nat Lofthouse one day, Puskás and Hidegkuti another. In winter when there was snow this same route would be fraught with danger for one could never tell from which direction a snowball would suddenly and painfully implode upon one's unsuspecting head. Then the entire walk could well transform into one continuous snowfight.

If all else failed, then I could always look forward to reaching one particular shop on Mackworth Road. It was a tiny, nondescript shop, its diamond-paned window jutting slightly out onto the pavement. It sold an assortment of things that were of no interest to me; the main attraction was its display of photographic magazines. Each morning as I went by, I would stand on tiptoe and peer through the glass and gaze avidly at small magazines, the covers of which displayed naked women. They were, in fact, photographic studies in black and white of the female nude. My first clear idea of the whole female body, and its demystification, I owe to these concentrated, voyeuristic peeks through that shop window.

It was on this route that I first encountered a large, fat, adenoidal, bespectacled boy of about fourteen or fifteen from the orphanage next to Ashgate. For a month or two he became my tormentor.

The orphanage was an object of intense curiosity to the students of Ashgate. Perhaps it conjured up in our minds lurid scenes from *Oliver Twist*. It adjoined the school and was separated from it by a high wall and so it was mostly invisible, though the sound of children playing in its grounds carried over.

Every now and then, a wildly thrown or erratically kicked ball from the school playground would stray over the wall. This gave the more intrepid boys an excuse to climb onto the top of the wall to secure its return and cast an inquisitive glance around.

The same thing would happen each day. The boy from the orphanage, presumably on his way to Sturgess School, would stand legs apart and hands on hips in front of me like a cowboy instigating a showdown, and block my path. He would then taunt me, usually referring to the colour of my skin, make some further inane comment and then pass on. Other boys going by would stare curiously at us.

This ordeal ended one morning as abruptly as it began. My tormentor blocked my path as usual and then addressed me in a friendly tone, as if I was an old friend. I stared at him in astonishment. He offered no explanation for this volte-face, but from that day on I seemed to have acquired what was virtually an admirer, for every now and then, as we met on the street going in opposite directions, he would present me with small gifts – pencils, erasers, football cards, bubble gum.

Oddly, I came to like him. I no longer saw him as a menacing, threatening bully but rather I felt a kind of compassion for the boy. He appeared rather pathetic and forlorn. His fatness, his breathlessness, the large plastic-rimmed glasses, the bloated, freckled face, his dirty, uncut fingernails, the glisten of perspiration, all so threatening became simply symptoms of his vulnerability.

Then one day, several months later, he simply disappeared: I never saw him again.

9

Home and Away

Over the next several months David and I became almost insep-
arable. At first, we abided by some implicit rule to restrict our
friendship to school hours and not to extend it to our homes.
How this tacit agreement came about is hard to say. Perhaps it
was the result of a certain diffidence on both our parts.

The fact was that sometimes I felt ever so slightly embarrassed
by the way my parents spoke the English language. I could never
explain the cause of this feeling at the time. Later, much older, I
would be able to articulate what it was about their speech that I
thought sounded strange – not to my ear but (I was sure) to my
friends', especially those from Ashgate. Their speech involved a
combination of what my father called a 'cultured' accent, the
sometimes complicated, often archaic words they chose to use,
their elaborate, carefully crafted sentences, the absence of collo-
quialism, of even the mildest slang (I sometimes wondered if
they knew English swear words) – it was all this that made their
speech patterns so strange, and which vexed me in a vague sort of
way.

I was not to know that what they spoke was a version of the

genteel English the educated Bengali elite, the *bhadrolok* of Calcutta, learn to speak; except that in my parents' particular case, it had been self-consciously refashioned to conform to the 'standard' accent, tone and pitch they would hear in the speech of the English people they had come to know.

In our neighbourhood, this irked me less, perhaps because my father, known generally in the locality as 'Doctor' (in airy disregard of the British medical protocol which insisted that surgeons be addressed as 'Mister'), enjoyed the regard which medical men command everywhere. My parents were familiar figures.

With David Newman the situation was different. I quickly came to know enough about the texture of his home life to sense a massive chasm between our respective backgrounds: it was not just that our fathers did two vastly different kinds of job – David's father was a postman and mine an ear, nose and throat surgeon; I was also struck by how much at odds our home lives were. I got the impression that David's father did extra jobs over weekends to add to their income, and that David would help him out. Indeed, David was already a wage earner of sorts, for he collected old newspapers from people's homes and sold them to some dealer. This gave him his pocket money. My own parents would be horrified if I were to do something like this.

Tentatively, I put my hypothesis to the test. One Saturday morning when she was sending me across the road to buy some bread at Buxton's, the bakery, I suggested to my mother that every time she sent me to do a chore, I should get sixpence. She listened with a frosty look on her face and then replied, grimly, that I would get my ear boxed instead of sixpence. My job was to get on with my studies, she said, and warned me never to talk about earning money this way. The topic was never broached again.

Early in our friendship, David asked me if I could speak

'Indian'. I explained that there was no such language as 'Indian', that many different languages were spoken in India, that the language that I and my parents spoke was called Bengali. David waved aside such niceties. He wanted to know what the 'Indian' slang for 'fuck' was, and for 'prick', 'cunt' and the other usual words that made up our playground dirty talk. I confessed I did not know, but to save face I said I knew the Bengali word for 'shit' – and I pronounced it slowly as if it was an English word. David was delighted, and so were some of my other friends. As we walked along Mackworth Road from school to the Rec where we held our football and cricket matches, they would chant gleefully, David the loudest, for all to hear, the word I had taught them, happy that our sports teacher or the passers-by could not understand.

With all this in mind, I was at first hesitant about inviting David home – not that I thought my parents would object, for I did not think that would be the case – but rather I feared that David might ridicule them because they were so 'different'.

Eventually, the barrier fell. Our need for each other's company was too compelling. We needed to talk football on weekends, to review the results as soon as they came out; we wanted to go to the Baseball Ground together on Saturday afternoons. I needed consolation when, on that Saturday evening in January, I stood at Dean's Newsagents, opened the *Football Special* impatiently, and looked in disbelief at the FA Cup third round scores. Blackpool 0–York City 2. History did repeat itself. Like Port Vale the year before, York was a Third Division team, but this time Blackpool lost at home. I walked back to our flat blindly, scarcely aware of my surroundings. At home, my parents were laughing and joking with Mihir-*da* and another of our Bengali friends. My father, blissfully unaware of my emotional state, invited me to play pick-a-sticks with him, a game we both took seriously and did not like to lose. I declined, of course. The contrast between their sense of bonhomie and my misery was unbearable. Life was terribly unfair. It was at moments like this that I wished I could talk to David. I knew that only he would understand.

Very tentatively we visited each other's homes. Frst David came to the Kedleston Road flat. I think he did find my parents a bit peculiar. He stared at my mother's sari, an attire he had never seen; he was taken aback by their speech. They talked to him softly, seriously, in their rounded, educated Bengali *bhadrolok* style – in the manner my father would speak to the children at the Children's Hospital. David must have found the contrast between my speech patterns and my parents' striking for he made some vague comment about it to me. But then, he was not to know that I had two versions of spoken English: there was the language I used in the company of my friends, when I talked to Harold or Pauline Amos or Graham or at school – indistinguishable in form from their Derby-Midlands English; and then there was the guarded, genteel language – vocabulary and speech – I employed in the presence of my parents and our Bengali contingent. In short, in footballing terms, I had a Home language and an Away language! In fact, I had a Home persona and an Away persona.

But David's street-smart toughness dissolved when he saw the model galleon my father had recently made. At that moment he became just another wide-eyed adolescent as he gazed, openmouthed, at the delicate wood carving on the ship's side, rigs woven from fine, red thread, sails fashioned out of parchment paper displaying emblems painted delicately in red, gold and black. He counted the guns, all twenty of them, protruding from each side, along the length of the boat. And all this, exquisitely held in a structure six inches long and eight inches high. I was pleased at David's excitement.

My father's model ship: a galleon and the Queen Elizabeth.

I had come to take my father's immense gift for granted, having watched him craft one beautiful thing after another with his slender, un-Bengali-white, delicate, almost effeminate surgeon's fingers ever since our days in Nottingham. Tulips made from coloured crepe paper of the sort used to make casings of birthday party crackers; gleaming black fireplace screens superimposed with bold, gold flowers vaguely Chinese in design, with matching coffee tables; small battleships made out of brown paper; a model farmyard complete with animals. One or another of these objects in a state of ongoing creation would always be lying around the flat. Prompted by the Hillary–Tenzing triumph, he had begun a large, scale model of Mount Everest, about two-and-a-half-feet square on the base and four feet high. He planned to finish it by Christmas so that it could be displayed in the ear, nose and throat ward at the Derbyshire Royal Infirmary. It would be made of plaster of Paris, and would show all the important peaks and the places where the recent expedition had made camp. It would have models of Hillary and Tenzing at the top – though they would not be to the same scale.

I approached my own maiden visit to David's home with some trepidation. The street and the neighbourhood reminded me of the approach to the Baseball Ground: the same endless rows of indistinguishable, red-brick dwellings, a skyline of chimneys, the same arid, treeless, deserted air, streets traversed by few cars.

David ushered me into his house not through the front door but the side gate. Every house on that street, in that neighbourhood, had one, of course. It opened into a short, dark, narrow passage which led to the garden at the back, a tiny square of straggly grass and shrubs, at one side of which, abutting the back wall of the house, was a small shed used to store their coal supply. We entered the house through the back door; this opened

My father's model of Mount Everest.

into the kitchen. Soon, I came to realize that the kitchen was the centre of their home life. They did not use the front living room; nor did they often open the front door. Almost all they needed for the conduct of their daily lives, save for washing, bathing and sleeping, was in that kitchen.

My apprehension was unfounded. Mrs Newman welcomed me with a smile. She said she had heard a lot about me 'from our David'.

Our David! I loved hearing this phrase, there was something warm and protective and possessive and tribal about it. 'Their Alf is going out with our Jenny', I might overhear on the bus, and I would imagine a cocky young man (an 'Alf'), perhaps chewing gum, leaving a house with a wispy-looking girl (a 'Jenny') on their first day of courtship, while Jenny's mother and sister would peer, inquisitively and excitedly through front-room curtains. From that day, for the next year and a half, I would spend more of our spare time in that house than anywhere else, except, perhaps, at my old friend Graham Dean's house.

In a sense, Graham and David also represented a Home and an Away – for Graham belonged to an older, more familiar, Kedleston Road-neighbourhood milieu. Most times I kept these lives separate, for they seemed separate. Besides, my hope that I could bring my 'old best friend' and my 'new best friend' together was dashed quickly. They simply did not like one another.

Pauline and Stanley's wedding was our first English wedding; for my parents, it was their first church service in England. My mother's sari, with its brilliant colour and elaborately patterned border, drew many curious stares, for Derby had few Indian women in its midst, and the sari was, for most of its denizens, a novelty.

I had yet to come to terms with the way people stared at my mother, as my nun-teachers and classmates had done in

Nottingham. On the bus, the women, in their dull headscarves and shapeless coats of uncertain age, would devour my mother with darting, hungry eyes as if she were a freak; on the street, shoulders sagging with the weight of shopping bags, they would stop dead in their tracks just to get a look at her. Some would ask outright how she wore it, what was underneath. My mother, unruffled, would reply patiently, good-naturedly, and laugh to see me fret and fume at their ignorance and inquisitiveness.

Pauline's wedding took place in Derby Cathedral, and there, too, they stared as we took our places. The women in the pews whispered to one another. The sari's colours made their sedate pinks and lavenders and beiges look dowdy, something that gave me an immense, obscure and perverse satisfaction.

But my pleasure quickly abated, for all the women wore hats except my mother. I had warned her about this, but she had paid no heed at the time or had forgotten. Now, on my hissing insistence (for once I was in command) she hastily pulled the sari's *aachal* over her head like a headscarf.

Pauline came down the aisle on the arm of Mr Amos who, in formal attire, looked even more craggily handsome, more Gary Cooper-esque. But I could only stare worshipfully at Pauline.

The service began. Chagrined once more, I observed that my parents could not locate the first hymn, and although the congregation had already begun to sing, my parents were helplessly flipping through the pages. I hastened to help them but then, of course, since they did not actually know the hymn, they could only gaze sheepishly at the words, lips unmoving. I squirmed in embarrassment, certain that every one would notice. To compensate, I sang louder than I needed to.

After the wedding, as the cathedral cast a long shadow across the pavement and onto the street, the guests took the short walk up to where the reception was being held, in an inn built in Tudor times, where we ate and watched the other guests dance, for my parents did not know how to dance Western-style. When we were about to leave, I could only look up sadly at Pauline, who smiled brilliantly at us, shook our hands and stooped to kiss me on the cheek. As she did so, I saw for a brief moment her full white breasts and that, and the touch of her lips, made me flush all over.

I saw very little of Pauline after her wedding. It was as if there had been placed, abruptly, some physical barrier between her old life and her new. In Bengal (I knew from scraps of overheard conversation) they say that when a girl marries she becomes a part of, she belongs to, another family, the family of her in-laws, her *sasur-bari* – and a guest thereafter in her own parents' home. I wondered whether something similar happened here in England.

Gazing out of the sitting room or kitchen window I sometimes caught sight of her on the street below. She would wave and smile and I would wave back. But we did not meet much, so I rarely spoke to her. Sometimes I would hear her voice rising up from the ground floor as she and her husband entered.

Pauline's departure from my milieu was yet another instance of coming to terms with farewells. By now I was hardened to this experience. I could deal with it. What happened in football was quite a different matter.

Here, too, I had a Home and an Away life. Away meant Blackpool and, that season, I could only watch miserably from afar as Stanley Matthews and Stanley Mortensen and most of the other stalwarts who had helped win the Cup just two years earlier played one terrible game after another; at one dreadful time, reporters were mentioning the unmentionable: relegation. Somehow, they managed to return to their winning ways, and I said my own prayers to God, thanking him, when they managed to survive. Their names would roll effortlessly from my tongue, as I had their signatures in my autograph book: Allan Brown and Bill Perry and Tommy Garrett and Harry Johnston and Ernie Taylor and Jackie Mudie and George Farm and Hugh Kelly, and now there were some new youngsters, Jimmy Armfield and Roy Gratrix.

But God did not answer my prayers – or anyone else's for that matter – when it came to matters closer to Home. By Christmas, Derby County was destined for relegation. By April, relegation was a fact of life. There were moments of hope as new players were signed in desperation. We felt a shiver of excitement when Jesse Pye, once of the Wolves' FA Cup-winning team of 1949, who had scored one of the goals in that game, and once an England international, arrived on the scene. We went to see him play. But neither he nor anyone else could do much, and we could only look on silently, morosely, as Derby prepared to play in the Third Division the next season.

One morning, in April, on the Ashgate playground before the bell rang for the start of school, a friend called Bob Humpstone taught me a new phrase: he said that Stanley Matthews had 'run rings round' Scotland the day before. And indeed he had. That day two concrete pieces of history were made: Sir Winston Churchill resigned as prime minister of Great Britain; and Duncan Edwards, the Manchester United prodigy, became the youngest player to play for England at the age of eighteen and a half. Both faded away in my scheme of things as England demolished Scotland by seven goals to two as surely as Hungary had once demolished England.

I saw the match on television and my heart danced as Matthews weaved, sprinted and swerved his way through the Scottish defence and made virtually all the goals. Dennis Wilshaw of Wolves scored four of the seven but, like Edwards's debut, like

Churchill's departure ('finally', my father and Mihir-*da* triumphantly exclaimed), this scoring feat was beside the point. Matthews, who had turned forty two months earlier, was the point.

The end of the season – my second in English football – would have left me joyless but for this match. When Chelsea, with Roy Bentley, won the League, I felt nothing. On Cup Final day I should have been neutral and outwardly I was, but inside I bore Newcastle and their centre forward Jackie Milburn a deep grudge – for just four years before they had defeated Blackpool in the final because of Milburn's two goals. Besides, David admired Bert Trautmann hugely, he was his second favourite goalkeeper, so I had a sneaking desire for Manchester City to win.

I watched the game downstairs at the Amoses', settled into my usual position on the pouffe, and felt a momentary shiver of excitement as Manchester City walked out onto the pitch wearing tracksuits. They looked immensely smart! No one had ever done this before in the annals of the FA Cup, and so we were witness to the making of a small piece of history that afternoon. I think it was that sight which induced in me a peculiar longing to possess and wear a tracksuit.

To my dismay, and David's, Bert Trautmann could do little to stop Newcastle from winning. A joyless season tempered only by that fortnight of delight in December when England beat Germany and then Wolves defeated Honved, and the day Matthews 'ran rings round' Scotland.

Going to Ashgate School and getting to know David Newman had affected not just my life but my parents' also, in subtle ways. I earned a new kind of independence. I went to places I had not known about before meeting David. We clambered up desolate embankments and squatted perilously close to railway lines to 'spot' trains and cross their numbers off in our little train books.

We went into small woods tucked away in odd, unexpected nooks, mindless of the 'Trespassers Will Be Prosecuted' signs, where I learned about bird nesting from David. In fact I was quite inept at climbing all but the simplest trees, and so most of the time I would stand below, clutching a tin box while David clambered expertly up and got lost in the foliage, before descending triumphantly, a bird's egg or two of some beautiful shade and improbable pattern clutched precariously in his hand, which we would then gently place inside the cotton wool-lined box.

Likewise, observing my enhanced independence, my parents discovered that they, too, could do things they had not been able to do all these years. They discovered that they could go to the cinema when their whim dictated and watch whatever films they desired and not have to worry about me. They could even attend hospital parties together.

They even started to learn ballroom dancing. They would go two evenings a week for their lessons somewhere in town and return elated that they had mastered yet another step, first the waltz because it was the easiest, then the quickstep the next week, the foxtrot another. Returning home, they would immediately put on a gramophone record and try out the steps again in the sitting room while I would watch.

Our thoughts turned to the summer holidays. My father, fascinated by the sea, suggested Llandudno – his fantasy was to be a ship's surgeon and sail the oceans. And then I was swept away by my parents' suggestion: perhaps David might like to come with us.

David's eyes danced at the prospect. He talked to his parents, and they agreed.

Arrangements were made. My father and I went to the Newmans' house, escorted by David. To my surprise, instead of entering through the side gate as usual, we were ushered through the front door into the living room. This was clearly an exceptional day!

It was all briskly decided. My father gave them an estimate of expenses and said he would make the bookings. Mr and Mrs Newman agreed amiably. David and I were ecstatic.

For me that one brief summer week in Llandudno in Wales was an interlude of magic. We swam, of course, for I had finally learned to swim in the public baths in Derby, and I was anxious to show off my new skill. My distaste for the saltiness of sea water had not abated, but at least I did not have to swallow so much of it now. On wet, windswept mornings we played football on the beach. We talked, argued (the old unending debates: Matthews versus Finney, Hutton versus Compton), wrestled in the sand, walked and explored the region. We smirked and nudged each other whenever we saw lovers kissing, embracing, defiantly entwined. We stared furtively at sloping, sun-reddened breasts spilling out of skimpy swimsuits and skimpier bikinis. We looked curiously but with casual interest at girls of our own age, some of whom looked so sure of themselves. We told and retold each other salacious jokes and anecdotes in which Errol Flynn and Jane Russell from America and Sabrina from within England would inevitably appear. We kept track, from the newspapers, of the fortunes of the South African cricket team touring England. We listened on the radio to Ruby Murray's 'Softly Softly' that had just been released, and to older favourites like Nat King Cole's 'A Blossom Fell', and Kitty Kallen's 'Little Things Mean a Lot'. Before dinner, we examined together some just-published football yearbook and looked sorrowfully at the league tables and statistics, and the latest *Playfair* cricket annual which I had brought with me. That week, I realized how things might have been had I had a brother.

We returned to Derby by coach to be met at the station by

David's parents. The two fathers shook hands. Mrs Newman hugged me, and my mother hugged David. Mr Newman shook my hand and my father David's. Thank yous were exchanged, goodbyes said.

10

Eleven-Plus

Late that autumn, I had my first dream – or rather nightmare – about the 11-plus. It faded almost the moment I awoke, and all I remembered was being told by a grim-faced father that I had failed the exam. I woke to the sound of my own yelp of despair.

As the school year (and the football season) progressed, dreams about the 11-plus increased in frequency. They would usually linger for only a minute or two after I awoke, and I could rarely recall them afterwards. With one exception. That dream has stayed in my consciousness for ever.

I dreamed that the school football team was playing a match on the Rec. From my position as left half I had centred the ball into the opposition's penalty area, and one of my teammates, the one who fancied himself as Puskás, had deftly dragged the ball back away from the feet of a defender and then immediately, in the same smooth, flowing movement, shot the ball into the net, just like Puskás had done against England.

As I raised my arm in triumph, someone grabbed me from behind. It was the headmaster. I heard him say something but I could not hear it because of the cheering spectators. Then he shouted, that I had not got through my 11-plus.

I was paralysed in horror. I could not move my arms and legs, I felt as if they were weighed down with sacks of coal. I knew what this meant: I was doomed, as good as dead. I heard the headmaster say repeatedly that I should have paid more attention to schoolwork and less to football. My parents would now disown me, they had said that if I brought shame upon them before their Bengali friends, their English friends, their relatives back home, they would disown me.

I began to run in despair out of the park, towards the street. I sensed that the headmaster and my form teacher, Mr Morris, and David were all chasing me. I heard David shout that I should not worry, there would be another chance. But there is only one chance in the 11-plus, I shouted back, and began to sob violently.

I woke to the sound of my own cry of horror, and I lay there, staring up at the ceiling, feeling so spent that I could scarcely move. That morning I narrated the dream to my mother, who consoled me.

Most times the dreams were about failure, and in a way I preferred that because when I woke up, I could at least exult in relief. But the dreams of passing the 11-plus were ones that were hard to accept, for then my disappointment upon waking ('it was only a dream') was so great that I would simply lie there, my face buried in the pillow.

This was our final year in Ashgate. I was in Form 4A, and our teacher, Mr Morris, had a formidable reputation. For one thing, he called all the students by their surnames, unlike Mr Graham, our 3A teacher (or, for that matter, the headmaster or the other teachers I came to know). For the first time I could remember, I was addressed as Gupta in class, a strange sensation. Even my tormentor Miss Sullivan at Convent School had called me by my first name. Perhaps Mr Morris wanted to maintain a distance from his students. Perhaps this was his way of not becoming close to his students.

In class, he stood for no nonsense. This was the year in which we would take our 11-plus exam, and his job was to get as many of us through as possible. He made sure we knew exactly what was at stake. The lucky few who passed the exam went on with scholarships to the grammar schools, to O levels at sixteen and then, for a few of that few, A levels at eighteen, and for the elite of the few of the few, there would be university. All the others – the majority – would go to 'secondary moderns', really vocational schools. Some of them might have a second chance at thirteen (in the '13-plus'), but most would join the workforce at fifteen, as apprentices in the large engineering companies in town if they were lucky, or lesser employment if they were not.

These facts were familiar to most of us as we started the new school year, but the headmaster (in his beginning-of-year speech to the 4A class) and Mr Morris made sure we understood.

We were, there is no doubt about it, a bit afraid of Mr Morris; afraid yet fascinated, because he came to school on a motorcycle – one of the bigger Royal Enfield models. The boys noticed him when he entered the gates; and they noticed his departure. Boys speculated about his personal life, about his love life. There was a mystique about him.

As for the 11-plus, we never discussed it among ourselves. If as individuals the boys harboured hopes and fears about it, they kept them pretty much to themselves. We simply put on nonchalant faces and went on with our lives.

For me, it was very different. At home it loomed ever so large in my parents' minds that year. They worried about it even as they took it for granted that I would pass the exam – because the alternative was unthinkable. Failing the 11-plus was not an option in their minds.

If I consciously resented my parents' automatic expectation, I did not express it. I was aware that few of my friends had such parental pressure imposed upon them. But then, they were not from India, they were not from the Bengali *bhadrolok* culture. My parents' assumptions were no more presumptuous than those of countless *bhadrolok* parents back in Calcutta. Even then, I was aware that people like my parents back home took it as self-evident that their sons (primarily sons) would do 'well' in school, go to a 'prestigious' university, get a 'brilliant' degree, embark on a 'promising' career, and make a 'good' living. My parents' expectations were very much along this line of thinking. They saw no reason to revise or reconsider it in Derby, England.

As for university, the very concept was alien to most of my Ashgate friends. To most of them, university was a distant thing and vaguely connected to sports. It meant the Cambridge–Oxford boat race; it meant earning mysterious things called Blues in rugby, cricket and rowing; it meant the combined Universities XI playing three-day cricket matches on working days when most other young men were engrossed in making a living. Some of us remembered that May Day, the year before, when Roger Bannister broke the 'four-minute-mile barrier' on a track in Oxford. We may have noticed that Bannister, and his two pacemakers, Chris Chataway and Chris Brasher, were all university students. Thus, to the extent that any one of my friends thought about university, it was in terms of sports, not academic affairs.

Our teachers occasionally spoke of this university or that, but only in passing, as when they talked about the Lives of Great Men, as when Mr Graham in 3A spoke about Alexander Fleming once and about Albert Schweitzer another time. We never knew whether any of our teachers or the headmaster had gone to university.

That I made connections between the outcome of the 11-plus and universities, that I knew not just about Oxford and Cambridge but also Manchester University and Imperial College and Guy's Hospital, and Calcutta University, that I was aware that people sought to put strings of letters after their names, that these letters meant something – these realizations were entirely the outcome of my parallel Bengali life. Abbreviations such as 'MB, BS', 'M.Sc.', 'BE', and even professional diplomas, 'AMI Mech.E' and 'FRCS', were meaningful to me, for I would hear or overhear their mention in our living room, whenever the Bengalis dropped in. I came to know that a woman who once came to spend a weekend with us from Oxford, whose name was Sumitra Talukdar and whose family my mother's family knew well, was doing research for a degree called 'D.Phil.' My father told me that an older brother of his had a 'D.Sc.' degree from Calcutta University, a rare and difficult degree (my father said) for research he had done for almost ten years. My father's pride in my uncle's achievement made a strong impression on me. In fact, that was my first encounter with the idea of research.

But the 11-plus did not dominate my life. There were other matters. On my eleventh birthday I became the owner of my first bicycle, a maroon BSA model with the straight handlebars that were all the rage among the young. It was a present from afar – my maternal uncle, who was the managing director of India Cycle, a business owned by my mother's family, had arranged with his business associates at BSA in England for its delivery. It appeared on our doorstep by magic on the morning of my birthday. My mobility and, as a result, my perception of our proximate universe were dramatically altered that day. I no longer walked to school. I no longer had to cajole Graham to let me ride his bike.

David's house became so much closer. In the evenings, after school, I could wheel my machine out of the shed at the bottom of the Amoses' garden and become part of the group that hung about the streets on their bikes – or would ride en masse into Markeaton Park. I now belonged to an invisible club from which I had hitherto been excluded.

I set about embellishing my bike: I went with my friends to a bicycle shop somewhere off Mackworth Road, and bought bright orange ('tangerine' – for Blackpool) tape and wound it round the handlebars as I had seen others do. A dynamo was fitted on, and this would power the lamp in front; the traditional bicycle bell was distinctly passé among the boys (in present-day jargon, 'uncool') and was rapidly discarded for a kind of electrically operated siren, which emitted a hoot. On one of the diagonal crossbars I fitted two flask holders to carry sleek-looking plastic flasks.

My Home circle of friends had both contracted and extended. Harold Heldrich, the boy from next door, my very first friend in Derby, had outgrown me. He was seriously into girls, and would soon be out of Sturgess School and into a job. We had drifted apart, it was a very natural thing to happen, and if I was sorry this had happened, I did not have much time to dwell on it, because my social life had suddenly been enriched with a mix of old and new friends, almost all boys, one or two girls, all of whom lived within a hundred yards of one another.

One, of course, was Graham Dean whose house was on Wheeldon Avenue. On Bromley Street, parallel and adjacent to Wheeldon, lived Johnny Newton. On Kedleston Road itself, a few houses away from ours, on the other side of Wheeldon Avenue, was Robin Darbyshire. Across from him was Alan Potter's house. And further up Wheeldon Avenue were Tony and Pat Moore, brother and sister.

We became a 'group'. The boys would go to the Baseball Ground together, often stand, packed like sardines in the boys' section, to watch a tepid Derby County wallowing in the Third Division. We played football on Markeaton Park. On Sundays, there would be long bicycle rides – beyond the city's limits into the countryside, along, straight, ribbon-like Roman roads, and we would drink orange juice from our plastic flasks as we had seen Tour de France cyclists do. On rainy days, we played snooker or billiards at Alan's house or table tennis or Monopoly and other board games at Graham's. In Johnny's living room, we admired his mother's knitting machine, and I would wonder whether Mrs Newton would make a polo-neck jersey like the royal blue one she had knitted for her son. We played skittles in Tony and Pat's back garden. If he was in the mood, Tony, a pianist, would strike up a tune, 'The Ballad of Davy Crockett' or some other current 'hit'. On weekday evenings, if we felt lazy, we would simply lounge about on Wheeldon Avenue, near Graham's house.

We were still, then, primarily a boys-dominated group doing boy things, but the occasional presence of a girl or two added a slight edge of excitement to our evenings. Pat Moore was the one girl who most often joined us, accompanied at times by her friends. Pat's brother, Tony, the oldest of us, was already in pursuit of girls. And so, when in summer, Graham's blonde and very pretty cousin Charlotte came to spend a few days with his family, a very perceptible ripple of excitement ran through some of us; but only Tony had the self-confidence, the verve, to pursue her, and we watched, fascinated and envious, their mutual flirtations.

Sometimes there would be fallings out between us; sometimes the majority would 'gang up' on one of the group, for reasons that were entirely trivial (in retrospect) – and when that happened we could be immeasurably and unforgivably cruel to the object of our spite.

How does a group form when one is that age? How did this
group cohere? There were other boys and girls around us, some
of whom we knew quite well, who drifted in and out of our lives,
but none became part of 'us'. How did we come together?

There was no one central nucleus which grew in size by addition. Rather, there were already in place several separate strands
of friendship that somehow joined together.

Alan and Johnny were old friends, and a year my senior. They
had gone to Ashgate. Alan passed his 11-plus and was now at
Bemrose Grammar School, while Johnny went to Sturgess
Secondary Modern just up Kedleston Road. Oddly enough I was
only on nodding acquaintance with them when they were at
Ashgate. Graham, a year my junior, and I were linked from the
days when I was at Convent School, which he was still attending,
and in this sense he was the odd boy out. The siblings, Pat and
Tony, had known Graham for a long time. Pat was the same age
as Alan and Johnny; she, too, had attended Ashgate, had passed
her 11-plus and was now at Parkfield Cedars, the girls' grammar
school not far from where we lived. Tony was at Sturgess School,
and would leave shortly at fifteen to join the job market. Robin
Darbyshire was the loner among us; I met him through our
respective parents, for Robin's father, an academic, had struck up
an acquaintance with my father. Robin was two years my senior,
a former Ashgate student, and now in the second form at
Bemrose.

If these were the strands that coalesced into one, no single
compelling factor kept us together. Perhaps it was in part that we
shared interests in several sports and pastimes; perhaps, in part
that all but Graham were Ashgate-connected; perhaps, in part we
simply got along and could find the same funny side in things;
perhaps it was in part because we were drawn together to the
New Music.

The New Music. As we lounged about in one house or another
we listened to a strange sound called rock 'n' roll which, when I first
heard it, made all my favourites, the Dean Martin-Nat King
Cole-Bing Crosby-Ruby Murray-Kitty Kallen-kind-of-music pale
into insignificance. It swept over us, we were overwhelmed, as
we listened to a hoarse, raspy, smoky voice, a voice which one
would never imagine would have the guts to sing, the voice of a
man called Bill Haley, and the frantic, insistent, plaintive rhythm
of his band called the Comets. We played that one record 'Rock
Around the Clock/See You Later, Alligator' again and again and
hungered for more. In Graham's upstairs bedroom, overlooking
the garden, we watched with a curious kind of excitement as
Pat and one of her Parkfield Cedars friends, a girl called Carol,
danced in the tiny space between the bed and the desk to the
rhythm of rock 'n' roll, their pleated skirts whirling this way
and that.

Friends and friendships were not the only things that kept me
from brooding excessively about the 11-plus. Not having older
brothers, I had no opportunity to observe the advent of male
puberty at close quarters. This was very definitely a disadvantage
of only-childhood. No doubt had I been among my cousins in
Calcutta, I would have been wiser (more 'street-smart', in current
jargon). But I was not, and so I was ill-prepared for the first man-
ifestations of puberty. For a few days I dwelt in a state of pure
'blue' funk. I was sure that something dreadful was happening to
my body.

I never confided these things to my friends. I was too embarrassed. But I listened quietly to the others talk. I even dipped
furtively into my father's more accessible medical textbooks. In
any case, I soon learned to my huge relief that nothing untoward
was happening to me.

In one way or another, physical contact between the sexes had long been a source of mysterious attraction to me. Perhaps because it was totally absent in my presence in our own home – Indian parents would never publicly touch each other in that way, or embrace or kiss – I was drawn to the sight of even the most elementary physical contacts between a man and a woman – walking arm-in-arm, for instance – while more intimate embraces would compel me to frankly stare from a safe distance or look away embarrassed when seen too close. At the cinema I would be distracted by the proximity of amorous couples.

Despite my voyeuristic tendencies, I shrank from actually talking about sex with my friends – but they seemed to be less inhibited; and not just to talk but to explore, as when one afternoon in our living room, with my parents away somewhere, I watched with a mixture of fascination and consternation as two of the boys in our 'group' indulged in mutual manual stimulation. It was a shock to see what I was already regarding as the most private of private acts being shared between two people – in the presence of a third person! Another time, as dusk descended on Wheeldon Avenue, the conversation somehow shifted to the topic of kissing – to its mechanics, to the way lovers kiss. The boys, still gauche, still with no experience, wondered how it was done, for surely the noses must get in the way. Pat and her friend Carol volunteered to give a demonstration, and before we could react, to our amazement – and inner excitement – they kissed each other fully, lingeringly, on the mouth. They were so much more self-assured, more precocious, than us, than even Tony or Robin, the two oldest boys.

The one thing that distanced me from all my friends that year was Blackpool. They did not love Blackpool the way I did. They 'loved' Stanley Matthews, but it was a perfunctory sort of love, the sort people have for a National Treasure, for Shakespeare, Lord Nelson, Winston Churchill. But they did not – they could not – feel the tremors of excitement that coursed through me as the season progressed.

It began gloriously. Mortensen and Bill Perry, the outside left, were scoring goals galore. Jackie Mudie was scoring. Even Matthews scored a goal, against Arsenal. Then my world began to totter: Eddie Shimwell, their long-time fullback retired; Harry Johnston, the captain, retired; and then I felt totally depleted when Stanley Mortensen, the second most important man in my football life, departed for Hull City in a less strenuous lower division.

For a while I was inconsolable. I could not fathom why 'Morty' had to leave. I had not yet come to terms with the ageing process, with the fact that the electric speed with which he would dart down the middle and latch onto a centre from Matthews – that speed was inexorably decaying with the passing of years. I could not accept that as in life so too in football, change was the one constancy; that one player gave way to another; that the club superseded the individual. To make things worse, there was no one I could turn to, on whom I could unload my desolation. There was no one Blackpool fan within my ken. David Newman would have understood, but he could never feel what I felt.

I cannot recall whether I felt guilty or disloyal to Mortensen as the season progressed, and my interest re-focused on Jackie Mudie, Mortensen's successor as centre forward. I watched gleefully as his goal tally increased. Even the team's early exit from the FA Cup did not erase the glow of hope, of satisfaction that seeped through my very pores. There was a real possibility that Blackpool could be League champions.

By April, it had distilled into a race between Blackpool ('us') and Manchester United. They were the Young Turks, collectively, the *enfant terrible* of English soccer; they were Matt Busby's Babes and already some of them, Tommy Taylor and Duncan Edwards and Roger Byrne and Johnny Berry, were on the path to legend-hood.

We travelled by coach, my father, Graham and I, to Manchester for the most vital match of the season between the two sides, and everyone, it seemed to me, except the Blackpool fans, were willing the Babes to victory in this match, and with that win, the League Championship. Romantic England (I felt) was siding with youth against age: Duncan Edwards was eight-een, Stanley Matthews forty-one.

At Old Trafford, I felt, for the first time, that I was not alone. We were still a minority, the Blackpool supporters, in this vast, 62-thousand-strong crowd, but at least there were others of my kind!

We walked on air for a while as our team went ahead; our euphoria turned to anxiety when they drew equal with a Johnny Berry penalty; and then our collective heart sank when United forged ahead from a goal by Tommy Taylor, and we knew it was all over. The *Maestro* was scarcely seen that day – indeed, I had a better, longer glimpse of him outside the ground driving away after the match than on the park. Duncan Edwards, a giant of a child, snuffed him out.

Blackpool finished the season as runners-up. It was the year that almost was! Matthews, like Tom Finney who had also once come close, never did get a League Champions medal.

When the 11-plus results were announced I was least prepared for them. It happened on one of those rare spring days that prop-erly resonated with the mythical image of the season of spring. The cloakroom downstairs was unusually bare, shorn of its cus-tomary confusing forest of scarves, raincoats and school caps.

There was a class in progress, but I have no recollection of what we were learning. We may well have been dozing, some of us, on this languid afternoon, though at our great peril, with Mr Morris's sharp eyes constantly roving around the room.

In the middle of our lesson, the headmaster walked in, clutching a bundle of brown, official-looking envelopes. I cannot speak for my classmates, but as my eyes focused on the headmaster's hands, and I realized the significance of the envelopes, I sat absolutely still. All the hackneyed phrases I had read in my adventure books, the Hardy Boys mysteries, *The Thirty-Nine Steps*, the Agatha Christies I had begun to read – blood freezing in the veins, chill running down the spine, hair standing on end, heart missing a beat, time coming to a stop – they raced pell-mell through my head. Later, I would think, they were all true, those things really happen, for they happened to me, inside me, all at the same time.

As the headmaster began to call out the names on the envelopes, one by one, I sat rigid, fists tightly clenched. With the announcement of each name I would hear a kind of swishing sound, of relief, of delight, issue from its owner.

As far as I could see, ten names had been called. The lucky ones clutched their precious envelopes. There was only one left in the headmaster's hand. The class was very still. It passed through my head, absurd though it was, that eleven of my class had passed the 11-plus – a coincidence which, in the midst of my tension, seemed just right; any occurrence of the number eleven would catch my attention. For me, it was a magic number.

The headmaster's gaze wandered slowly round the classroom. It reached me and paused. Our eyes made contact and then, almost imperceptibly, his eyes drifted away. I felt empty, blank, defeated. I thought of my parents and the impending disgrace. But then, the headmaster's eyes swept back and came to rest once more on me, and we looked again at each other in the eye and, feeling sick, I saw his eyes crinkle, and the ruddy face relax into a broad smile. I heard from a great distance my name being called, not 'Subrata', not 'Gupta', but my nickname, 'Poupeé', and the tension which had gripped the entire class was all at once released. Belatedly, as he handed over the envelope to me, I realized that he had been teasing me, had kept my name for the last. I knew that the headmaster had a soft spot for me though I had no idea why. I realized that this was his way of showing his affection.

The tightness in my stomach vanished miraculously, as also the urge to relieve my bowels. I felt light-headed, jubilant, slightly 'barmy' as I cycled back home with my precious envelope. I could visualize my parents' faces when they heard the news. They would both shed tears of relief, my father silently, in the stifled, uncouth way grown men cry, my mother unashamedly, with long, loud sobs.

Yet, as I pelted down the staircase two at a time and out into the warmth of the afternoon sun, my jubilation was mixed with another sensation – of sadness or unhappiness, I was not sure. So many of the others – most of the class 4A and, of course, all of 4B and 4C, had not passed.

David had congratulated me, slapped me on the back and said he had 'known it all the time'. He was neither surprised nor especially unhappy with his own result, for he harboured few expectations of success for himself; he was usually ranked in the bottom half of the class at the end of each term, a fact he accepted with aplomb, being far more preoccupied with football, cricket and (though somewhat less frequently) fighting than classwork. He was content that he had played goalie in the school football team and had represented the school in cricket.

As for his parents, even then, even at that age, I had sensed a quiet resignation on their part about what kind of life their son would lead. Their hopes and ambitions for David were so modest that listening to them talk even I, at eleven, was struck by its stark contrast to the confident, presumptuous expectations my own parents nurtured on my behalf. I would feel guilty, and the question of telling them what my parents hoped for me did not arise.

In one term, David did unexpectedly well, rising above his usual rank in class. I observed my friend's surprised pleasure and rejoiced with him. David insisted that I should accompany him home, to be there when he showed his report card to his parents. I saw their eyes light up. Perhaps they had even harboured unthinkable thoughts of improbable possibilities. The next term David returned to his customary rank and resumed his old, phlegmatic self.

Cycling home, I was reminded of that brief time when my cynical, tough-talking, self-mocking friend, and perhaps his parents, had experienced hope. I could not help feeling an odd sense of disquiet, of there being something terribly wrong about it all.

That evening, and in the days after, I was not able to decipher what exactly it was that was troubling me. That would come much later, when I began to ask myself questions about race and class and the perpetuation of class structure through the English system of education.

It was only then that I recognized how easily – how horribly easily – I myself could have missed the privileges I had come to take for granted. I realized then, and was appalled at the thought, that the possibility of knowledge and its denial – that who shall have and who shall not have access to knowledge – were determined on behalf of hapless children each year based on an examination taken at an age when one scarcely had any inkling of what was at stake. I would be filled with anger, bafflement, a dark kind of wonder and astonishment at how a nation could delude itself into such a way of thinking.

Many years later in another time and another place I would read in the *Manchester Guardian* that the 11-plus examination had been abolished. I would sadly recall my friend David Newman and all those others, those countless boys and girls who trooped noisily and cheerfully past our flat on Kedleston Road each day, to and from the secondary modern schools nearby. Would it have made a difference to their lives, I wondered, had they gone to school in these new times? Had a whole generation of kids failed the 11-plus in vain?

There was another cause for my sense of disquiet. As I wheeled my bike out of the school ground, and David and I went our separate ways, I realized – and sensed that David must also have realized – that the summer just ahead might be the last time we would spend together. My feeling was purely intuitive and unformed. And I did not understand how or why it should be so. I was not to apprehend that very soon, in the coming autumn, the chasm between our respective horizons would far overwhelm our present bond, a bond created on an absurdly intense, shared passion for the game of football.

We did meet often that summer. We went to see the Derbyshire cricket matches at the County ground and in Chesterfield under the shadows of its crooked spire. The Australians were in the country, and we exulted in what was very definitely Jim Laker's Ashes, as he spun them dizzy. Yet each time David and I met that summer, we seemed to have less to talk about, as if we had consumed our quota of friendship in these two intense, halcyon years.

When autumn came and we entered our respective schools, we would run into one another every now and then, but these encounters tapered off and, by Christmas, I scarcely spared a thought for David. Several months later, playing football on Markeaton Park on a frosty March morning, I looked up and spotted David on the touchline. He was even taller than before and looked stronger; he had a new hairstyle. And he was wearing the familiar green and yellow scarf of Ashgate School. Seeing him so unexpectedly threw me off balance.

I walked over during a lull in the play. We said hello to one another; David grinned at me, the same old defiant, insolent grin, yet oddly twisted. Then play resumed, and I got caught up in it. When I had the chance to look up in his direction, he was gone.

11

A Certain Strain

At some point in our life in Derby, I recall a startling letter arriving from a relative in Calcutta. From what I understood as a result of some intense eavesdropping on my parents' excited conversation, it spoke of three brothers, remotely related to us, who had been arrested on the charge of murdering their landlord. Apparently, there had been a long-standing dispute over water between the brothers, who lived with their families on the upper floor of a house, and their landlord, who occupied the ground floor. A few days before, our relative wrote, a very loud and verbally violent altercation occurred outside the house, witnessed by neighbours, and one of the brothers was heard to make a threat that if the water supply to their flat was not increased, the landlord would regret it.

Soon after that, the landlord was found dead, and though he had apparently died of a heart attack, the police suspected foul play because of what the neighbours told them they had heard and seen. The brothers were arrested.

The newspapers in Calcutta apparently wrote much about the court trial. Eventually, the brothers were found not guilty and released.

Landlords and tenants. This was a fundamentally doomed relationship, especially in India, as I would learn later. Poems were composed about it, novels were centred around it, movies were made of it, history was full of it.

It was also a theme which, coincidentally, had been intruding uneasily into our lives of late. Even I, preoccupied as I was with other matters, self-absorbed as I was, began to notice a certain strain within the house at 108 Kedleston Road.

At first, the change was barely perceptible. I heard my father say to my mother that, perhaps, they were simply imagining things. Eventually, they were both forced to acknowledge that there was indeed something very wrong.

Even at that age, I was vaguely aware of a tinge of the improbable about my parents' relationship with the Amoses: a friendship between landlord and tenant; between surgeon and porter; between bus conductress and the daughter of a proud, prominent, upper-class Bengali family. Yet, a very genuine, easy-going, undemanding affability had developed between my parents and the Amoses. It strengthened as time went by. My parents' sense of alienation had never completely vanished in the years they had been in England, but to a great extent it had been diluted by their friendship with Mr and Mrs Amos. In her bouts of almost maniacal homesickness with which my mother was afflicted, it was the conviviality within our house that helped to sustain and console her.

My parents occasionally went downstairs in the evening, and I would hear the sound of laughter, the tinkle of the piano, for Pauline used to play it, and so did Mr Amos. Indeed, spontaneous bursts of music and song were prominent features of our house – whether it was my mother upstairs or Pauline playing below (especially before her marriage) or Mr Amos, who had a fine tenor voice. Even with our living-room door shut, his voice would come to us, with fragments of his favourite songs, Nat King Cole's 'Answer Me My Love', or Ruby Murray's 'Evermore', or the haunting lines of 'Unchained Melody'. And if not singing, we would hear him whistling, loud and clear and sweet.

My mother taught Mrs Amos how to wear a sari, and they posed together for pictures my father took. Mrs Amos taught my mother to make Yorkshire pudding, a favourite of mine that I wanted to eat at home and could not till my mother learned how to make it.

On Sunday afternoons, when it was really summery, they would walk to Markeaton Park together, my parents and the Amoses, to the lake, where they would rent a boat and the men took turns to row lazily round and round the lake, while their wives leaned back on waterproof plastic cushions, trailed fingers through the water, and nibbled ice-cream cones. Sometimes, I would spot them from a distance, as we played cricket, or were making a nuisance of ourselves on our bicycles and – disturbing – entwined bodies of couples lying on the freshly cut, sweet-smelling grass.

My father and Mr Amos began to 'do' the football pools together, and swapped dreams of what they would do were they to hit the jackpot. That never happened, but one memorable Saturday evening, matching the results of the matches announced on the radio against their forecasts, the two men were thrown into a paroxysm of excitement because their forecasts had been correct – until it was discovered that Mr Amos had for-gotten to mail the pools coupons that week! Their chagrin and the chagrin of their wives were, predictably, huge. They moaned the next week through. The only success they ever had on the pools was to win five pounds once.

On one occasion they drove together in the Amoses' Vauxhall Velox to Dove Dale in the Peak District.

I had been to Dove Dale before, once with our Bengali and other Indian friends, another time with a group of boys and girls including the Heldriches from next door. I remember that trip well: soon after we reached there, Harold disappeared with a girl somewhere on those craggy hills, and I did not see him again till it was time for us to catch the train back. I still looked up to him – not only because he was several years older, not only because he was the first to befriend me when I came to Derby, but also because he played football far better than I could. Harold was, of course, sublimely unaware of my misery at being abandoned. I knew then that our friendship was about to dwindle.

I went with my parents and the Amoses very reluctantly because my mother insisted, and I sulked all the way. But once we reached Dove Dale and I began to climb the steep, rocky slopes of a substantial hill, my grouchiness evaporated.

The first time I had climbed a hill, I was very small, about five. We still lived in India, and had gone, all the cousins and our mothers, for a winter holiday to a place called Dhanbad, a provincial town in Bihar's coal-mining district. Later, many years later, I would revisit this town and faint memories of unusual sights and sounds would be revived. Here, instead of thronging crowds on cement pavements as in Calcutta, there were only strips of sand lining the roadside, used mostly by the local tribal, *Santhal* women, with baskets of goods on their heads on their way to and from the market, dark-dark-brown-complexioned, straight-backed, sharp-eyed, breasts shivering impudently beneath thin, grey saris; where, instead of sweat-encrusted, emaciated, panting men pulling rickshaws running barefeet like horses pulling carriages, they sat in dignity on seats and pedalled their three-wheeled cycle-rickshaws.

That first time, we had gone to stay with one of my uncles, my father's third oldest brother and his wife. They lived in a huge multi-roomed, sprawling bungalow belonging to the Indian School of Mines where my uncle was Professor of Chemistry and Metallurgy. The bungalow was so large that most of its rooms were empty unless they had guests. One spare room was 'occupied', however, by a dozen or more earthen images of the goddess Saràswati, remnants and reminders of past *Pujas*. We cousins all felt eerie when we entered that room; it was as if a dozen women – each identically attired, each holding an identical stringed musical instrument, each accompanied by a swan, each with the same half-smiling, half-stony look on their identically beautiful faces – had been held prisoners for so long that they had turned to stone. When I first visited Madame Tussaud's in London, I was reminded of this congregation of Saraswatis.

At the back of the house was a dense wood filled with guava trees, and from the obscure reaches of the wood at night, we would hear the curious, yelping howling of jackals. In the front, facing the road, was a splendid, red-gravel courtyard from where we could see in the distance dark, purple hills which every one of the cousins longed to climb. And so, one early morning, when the air was still clothed in a grey-blue, pre-dawn haze, the cousins, myself included, and the more adventurous of our mothers and aunts, silently slipped out of the house. The older cousins walked to the foot of the hill we wanted to climb, while the rest, shepherding the youngest ones, prodded awake the cycle-rickshaw wallahs who slept on the seats of their vehicles not too far from the house, and persuaded them to take us there.

In Dove Dale, I hazily remembered that day, as I climbed slowly to the top and stood there in the pose of Sherpa Tenzing.

We picnicked by the waterside, by the River Dove itself, mainly off sandwiches, scones, orange juice and lemonade, and the flask of tea that my father found indispensable.

My mother would become very pensive whenever we went on picnics, which we often did in summer, mostly with our Bengali and other Indian friends who came to stay with us for a weekend or a few days; these could be visitors from Calcutta, from London, the odd university student from Oxford or Imperial College, sometimes my father's medical friends, sometimes my mother's old classmates; and this time was no exception. And I knew the reason.

I knew that on such days she was reminded of winter days in Calcutta, in late December or early January, when her people, the Gupta family, would go on picnics. My maternal uncle, my mother's older brother, did things in style; he liked to do things differently. Sometimes he would rent an open lorry, the kind that Calcutta police used to transport its constables, with skeletal metal frames, ends attached to the deck forming inverted Us. The lorry would start its journey at my mother's parental house, the house of the Gupta family, at 47 Theatre Road – where I was born – and wend its way through Calcutta, stopping at various houses to collect the married daughters of the family – whose surnames had changed from Gupta to something else, like Majumdar, Roy, Sen, Dasgupta, all the usual surnames of the *Vaidya* community to which they belonged – and their husbands and children.

The lorry would arrive at our house almost last, because it was the farthest away from Theatre Road, tucked away in a side lane in north Calcutta, not far from the University College of Science. My parents and I would climb onto the lorry, already packed chock-full, and it would then make its way to its destination, very often to Kidderpore, where we would board a steamer to cross the Hooghly (as the Ganges is known where it passes through Calcutta) and deposit us on the other side of the river, at the Botanical Gardens, a very popular picnic site.

Whenever my mother talked wistfully of those days, I, too, would conjure up fragmentary but vivid images of those lorry journeys. In between tears and laughter, she would reminisce how her mother and all her aunts, who otherwise led the most measured lives in the great house on Theatre Road, would, on these occasions, shed their stately dignity; they, too, would climb onto the lorry, accompanied by cries of physical effort and a great deal of shouting and laughter and assistance from their vast number of offspring. Along with their sons and daughters and sons-in-law and daughters-in-law and nephews and nieces and grandsons and granddaughters and grandnephews and grand-nieces, they would stand on the deck of the lorry, clutching onto the metal frames, for all the world to see them. On that lorry, as it shook and rattled its way through the city, they, too, shed their inhibitions. They would gaze back, unconcernedly, at the people we passed, who looked in curiosity and surprise at the unusual sight of thirty or forty well-dressed men, women and children in a battered lorry, often singing tunefully (for my mother's family was exceptionally talented in music) at the tops of their voices, one song after another – perhaps a hit Hindi film song or one of Tagore's blood-coursing patriotic songs.

How or why things began to change in Derby I was not to know then, but it seemed to begin some time after I entered Bemrose Grammar School. Later, my father would say that the Howells had something to do with it.

The Howells came to occupy the attic flat upstairs in my last year at Ashgate. They were Welsh, newly married, in their late twenties perhaps or early thirties, and came to Derby right after their honeymoon, with teaching jobs in a local college. So far as I recall, they were both music teachers. They were a handsome couple, the Howells, and I was a bit smitten with Mrs Howell's pretty looks. Learning they were from Wales, I took the earliest opportunity to quiz Mr Howell about his knowledge of Welsh footballers, especially John Charles and Ivor Allchurch. Mr Howell had a lovely singing voice, and the whole house would know he was back from work, for he would climb the two flights of stairs singing at the top of his voice, unaffectedly, unconstrainedly, whatever took his fancy. His favourite, it seemed, was 'The Man from Laramie', though he would sometimes delight me with his rendition of 'The Ballad of Davy Crockett' long after the craze for this song had died out.

For quite some time my parents got along famously with the Howells, who were keener than most of our English acquaintances to learn about India. Mrs Howell tried on a sari with my mother's help. They would come down to our flat and chat on cold evenings, huddled as close as they could to the coal fire, our only source of warmth in the living room. I would also spend time with them in their tiny attic bedsitter. When she heard I loved apple pie, Mrs Howell would call me upstairs whenever she made one. I would then think of the Thomases in Nottingham. Once, when my mother complained to Mr Howell about the kind of books I was reading, that instead of *Huckleberry Finn* or *Tom Sawyer* or *Uncle Tom's Cabin* I would spend hours on the Billy Bunter stories, he defended me by assuring her that Frank Richards's literary style was not that bad, really. My mother was visibly taken aback, and I cast a grateful glance at my saviour.

Nonetheless, she was exasperated as to why I was so resistant to these particular works which she was, apparently, so keen for me to read. It was only later I realized the reason: I could not identify with the American classics. I never have. It exasperated her even more that I was quite happy to consume the Hardy Boys adventure tales of modern New England. Even in these, purely escapist stories, American affluence shone through: the fact that

My mother and Mrs Howell (left).

the Hardy Boys owned and rode motorcycles at the age of fifteen or sixteen impressed me no end. But not the classics.

The Howells began to spend their evenings with the Amoses, presumably for drinks. My parents were, in this matter, very traditional Bengalis: the nearest drink to alcohol for them was cider, and so they were naturally excluded from such occasions.

It was about this time, when the Amoses and the Howells began to spend more of their evenings together, that the trouble began.

At first, there were only the smallest signs of things not quite right. Even I noticed things. Greetings of 'good morning' and 'good evening' without the usual smiles; no cheerful yell from the foot of the stairs from Mr Amos inviting my parents down to watch television. Sometimes, we would hear, percolating up through the floor, scraps of cheerful chatter, their voices, the Amoses' or the Howells', snatches of songs, and the mellifluous tinkle of the piano.

Then one evening I came home to find my parents sitting very still in the living room. My mother's face was ashen, my father's drawn, and he was pinching his lips with his thumb and forefinger as he always did when perturbed. They did not say anything to me directly but over the next two days, listening to them, eavesdropping on them, straining to hear what they said to Mihir-*da*, I pieced together what had happened.

Apparently, Mrs Amos had complained about our 'excessive' use of electricity and water, much more than what my father paid for as part of the rent. My mother, bewildered and shaken, said she had never heard Mrs Amos speak in this curt fashion before.

Then one lovely autumnal Monday, as the sun's warmth dissolved the early morning chill, I found pinned to the wall in the bathroom we all shared, above the sink, next to the mirror, a poster. A stern face which I recognized as Stalin's stared out at me and underneath, it said in large crayoned letters

BIG BROTHER IS WATCHING YOU

My first reaction was that it was an obscure joke which I did not understand. I was flummoxed by the 'Big Brother' phrase. It was not a typical English term so far as I knew – rather, it was a literal translation of the Bengali word *dada* (or *-da* for short, as in Mihir-*da*) and I wondered, somewhat absurdly, whether someone, Mr Howell, perhaps, had learned it from my parents and put it up in some playful gesture. But who was 'Big Brother', and why should he, whoever he was, be watching me or anyone else for that matter? And what was the connection with Stalin?

My parents were as mystified as I was. They could not decipher the message. They had no idea what 'Big Brother' meant. But I could see that they were disturbed. As I left the house from the back door, satchel on my back, and wheeled my bicycle out of the shed in the garden, I, too, felt distinctly queasy in my stomach and bowels. I could not stop thinking of the cryptic sentence and the image of Stalin's gaze.

Then, one day, perhaps a week later, the poster disappeared as suddenly as it had appeared.

Years later, in my first year in college, I was sitting alone at a table in Calcutta's most famous coffee house, drinking cold coffee, and reading *Nineteen Eighty-Four*, when my mind raced back to that poster and those words and the term 'Big Brother' I had not understood. The penny finally dropped. I realized then, that whoever had put up the notice, had done so with malice aforethought.

The Sunday afternoon summer walks to Markeaton Park, the lazy boatings on the lake, tailed away. My father and Mr Amos no longer did the football pools together. They had not stopped talking to one another; on the surface, they were still cordial in a polite, frigid sort of way, but their interchanges had reduced to the smallest of small talk. The occasional afternoon women-talk, which Mrs Amos (when she was off duty), my mother, and Mrs Howell (when not teaching) had indulged in, had stopped.

My parents were at a loss to explain what had happened. Of course, they consulted their friends. One of my mother's close English friends was a woman named Joyce of whom I was very fond. She lived quite close to us, at the top of Statham Street, one of the many quiet streets off Kedleston Road, and in my last year at Ashgate, she had tutored me to prepare for the 11-plus.

Joyce was an Indophile and an active member of the Derby branch of an association called the International Friendship League, and I think we had come to know her through Mihir-*da*, who had met her at one of their meetings. Later, much later, I would run into Joyce in a shoe store in Calcutta; she did not recognize me till I introduced myself, and her first words were that I had lost my 'lovely' Derby accent; I could hear the reproach in her voice. By then she was Joyce Bose, having married into a hugely eminent Bengali family: her husband was the nephew of the great Indian Nationalists of the pre-Independence era, Netaji Subhas Bose and his brother Sarat Bose.

In our living room, as I sat looking through and sorting my collection of football match programmes – I had built up a massive collection and was constantly acquiring new ones by writing to football clubs all over England and asking for programmes of past matches, which they would obligingly send – I would overhear endless speculations by my parents, Mihir-*da* and Joyce about the Amoses' volte-face.

Perhaps beneath their liberal exterior, the Howells were inherently racially prejudiced, and had sown seeds of discord in the

Amoses' minds, they thought. Perhaps it was a case of the Howells and the Amoses, two of a kind, white, British, just 'ganging up' against another who was not of their kind. Perhaps it was the smell of Bengali cooking which even our Bengali visitors immediately noticed, however faintly, when they entered the house; it could be, they conjectured, that the Amoses had first got used to it until the Howells brought it to their attention; or out of politeness they had silently endured the odour till a chance remark by the Howells triggered an outpouring of pent-up resentment. Perhaps it was the sound of continuous chatter in an incomprehensible language which had irritated them over time, as one often is irritated by the insistent sound of a tongue one does not know. Perhaps it was the fact that my mother never wore a dress but always a sari; perhaps this had created an obscure distance, a heightened sense of 'us' and 'her', had made the women resentful over time. Perhaps, they thought, helplessly, it was all these tiny, petty, ordinary things acting in concert.

12

New World

If pressed, I would have been perplexed to state what precisely I expected of my new school. Perhaps I had a mental model of higher English schooling vaguely tinged with accounts of school life gleaned from ample readings of Frank Richards's Billy Bunter stories. Perhaps I carried images of quadrangles and tuck shops; of house matches and cross-country races; of academic gowns flapping in the wind; of languid afternoons on the cricket ground; and tall, thin, serious and responsible sixth-formers about to leave school. Not that I seriously believed, or thought my friends believed, that real grammar schools were ever like the fictional Greyfriars – just as I never took seriously the notion that on holidays in summer or winter one could actually get embroiled in adventures of the Arthur Ransome *Swallows and Amazons* kind.

I fully recognized – and I am sure that my more bookish friends also did – that these adventures, those school stories, were simply abstractions, reveries pleasant to contemplate; but never to daydream about. We no more sought or pined for such worlds than we, who read Agatha Christie, sought St Mary

Mead-like villages when we went on bicycle rides out into the countryside.

Years later, in another world, I would sit slouched at a table in a coffee house in Calcutta. Oblivious to the clatter of cups on saucers, the chatter of raucous voices, the laughter, the strident, sporadic yells from one table to another, the fragments of flirtations that would waft by, and the ever-present haze and smell of cheap cigarette smoke, I would read George Orwell's essay, 'Boys' Weeklies'.

I was at once amused and irritated. Amused because the essay triggered memories of stories and once-familiar characters almost forgotten. Yet, much as I admired Mr Orwell, my amusement was tempered by what I felt was the author's patronizing, supercilious tone, his glib generalizations about what makes the 'masses', the petite bourgoisie, tick when they read these schoolboy stories.

I wished I could summon Mr Orwell and sit him down at my table. I would tell him that I flatly disagreed with him; that I was one of those middle-class slobs, of whom he wrote so patronizingly, who no more identified with the characters of the posh, fictional public schools described in those stories than I later identified with Lord Peter Wimsey or Albert Campion.

I wanted to take issue with Mr Orwell who thought that those public-school stories induced a kind of 'wealth fantasy' in its readers. I would have said: 'That's nonsense, money meant nothing to us then.'

Of course, we were fascinated, we even coveted, material things of a particular kind: twelve-speed, derailleur gear, lightweight bicycles, the new 33-rpm LPs and 45-rpm EPs that had just appeared, dark maroon tracksuits with white piping down the sides. But then, the public-school stories we read had very little to say about such things. If anything, we were more fascinated by the technology of the modern American adventure tales.

I must have stared absently at the pretty, doe-eyed girl at the next table and caught her eye, for she made a face and hastily turned away. What would George Orwell say to me, I wondered. Something crushing, no doubt, in the manner of his hero in *Keep the Aspidistra Flying*.

Yet the school life I had mentally inhabited from those many hours on cold, wet weekend afternoons curled up with Mr Frank Richards's stories was not entirely missing at Bemrose. There were, indeed, cross-country running and inter-house rivalry, and tall, slim sixth-formers who were more men than boys. The teachers did wear gowns; there was a shop named 'Ye Olde Tuck Shop' just outside the school gates, where we would buy cinnamon buns. And there was a headmaster who looked and seemed, to my awestruck eyes, a man of learning.

Mr E. G. Bennett welcomed us the first morning at assembly. He was tall and spare and distinguished-looking, and I was reminded of an illustration of the title character on the dust jacket of one of my mother's favourite novels, Jean Webster's *Daddy-Long-Legs*. Years later, seeing Fred Astaire in this role in the film version, I would once more think of Mr Bennett.

I had already learned from my father that Mr Bennett was a Cambridge graduate. That first day, looking up at him on the stage in the school's imposing assembly hall, I found, at last, a link between my Away world and the elusive, almost semi-mythical notion of the scholar that I had come to know of in my Home world. At last I had found a man in the world out there who matched the scholar's image I had imbibed at home.

This image had evolved over time. My father would proudly tell me again and again that his third oldest brother, my uncle who was a professor at the Indian School of Mines, held a Doctor of Science degree from Calcutta University. He impressed upon me that this was a very difficult and rare degree. My mother had told me about her brother-in-law, my maternal aunt's husband who possessed a Doctor of Philosophy degree from the University of Heidelberg. One of our Bengali visitors was a woman studying for a Doctor of Philosophy degree at Oxford University. From these examples, I had built up a kind of scholar-figure image in my head.

But I knew no one out there who bore any resemblance whatsoever in what they did, what they said, to this image. Till that morning. In Mr Bennett – in his speech, his gravity, his distinctive appearance, the way he comported himself – I found at last an incarnation of this image.

On the first day, the new boys were instructed to visit the row of notice boards in the main corridor. I found myself in the midst of a milling crowd, craning my neck to read the announcements. One caught my special attention: I had been placed in Newton House.

My friend, Alan Potter, now a Bemrose veteran of one whole year, had taken me in hand, from the moment we reached the school gates. We wheeled our bikes to the bicycle shed where he showed me my proper section. He now told me that I would have Bob Wilson as my house captain; he said that Mr Norville was my house master.

School houses! House captains! House masters! A school motto in Latin! I could not have expected more. As Alan and I went outside and he escorted me to the back where the playing fields lay, my exhilaration knew no bounds. Had this been a more typical English day, had it rained or been cloudy, had it been cold, perhaps I would have felt differently. Instead, it was the kind of autumn morning we long for, the kind that lingers in our minds for ever, the kind we associate with a blue-grey morning haze, with the faintly acrid but not unpleasant tang of smoke which hangs in the air when someone, somewhere burns dead autumn leaves. It was the kind of autumn day you want to clutch and not let go of. It was the ideal day for new beginnings.

In the distance, I could see goalposts gleaming in the sunlight. They looked newly painted. And there were so many of them. My heart danced at the sight. I turned to look at the long, two-storey school building trisected by two tall towers. I looked at Alan and smiled. I had entered a New World.

Alan gave me a hasty tour of the school. We paused in the library and I caught my breath at the sight of books row-upon-row. We poked our heads into the changing room. Back in the hall where we had had morning assembly, he pointed out the organ at the back and the gallery where the school choir took their place each morning.

Several of my Ashgate classmates, other successful 11-plus-ers, had also come to Bemrose, and we exchanged greetings, like long-lost brothers, grateful to spot a few familiar faces. Their faces and personas have stuck firmly in some obscure recess of my memory and can be summoned at will; their names have partly faded with the passing of years, corrupted, perhaps a letter here and a letter there have been mutated like genes in one's DNA during combination. Yet I can make the effort to recall: David Bushell, who once had a fist fight inside the classroom one wet lunchbreak with his cousin, was caned thereafter, and had cried noiselessly the whole afternoon in class – whether from the physical pain of his cousin's blows or the cane, we did not know; Graham Fowers, talkative, cheerful, who every now and then would sing in class under his breath a catchy little song called 'Pretty Little Black-Eyed Susie'. Andrew Simpson, unfairly branded by our classmates in Ashgate a 'teacher's pet', quiet, studious and lonely – who, for some reason, liked me and once invited me to his house for tea; Bob Humpston, small, earnest-looking, my one link with David Newman, for they had been friends long before I went to Ashgate; and Clive Bagley, usually the top student in our class in Ashgate, a bit Billy Bunter-ish in girth but not in intellect, who would constantly harangue me both in Ashgate and then in Bemrose for not wearing my glasses. There were others I recognized, former seniors, from Alan's batch in Ashgate; I was even reunited with a boy who had been in my class at Convent School.

It was all rather like one of those dreams in which you see yourself drifting across some foreign landscape. But every now and then, a known face floats by and you shout to him in delighted recognition. They provide, in your dream life, reassuring anchor points.

If an outside observer had somehow entered the Bemrose School premises, and followed the daily rites of school life – if, in particular, he had kept track of Bob Wilson's daily routine, he would surely have expressed silent wonder. He would have asked himself the question: what prompts a youth of seventeen or eighteen, a sixth-former like Bob, belonging to a breed apart from the rest of the school, looking towards university, women and careers, eschewing the indignity of school uniform for corduroy jackets and leather elbow patches, or snappy suits – why should someone like that give so much of his precious time to a gaggle of noisy, unruly twelve-year-olds? What drives him? Why does he do it?

I first met Bob Wilson at the welcoming meeting of Newton House. We gathered in a largish classroom on the first floor.

As I and the other first formers took our place self-consciously in the front, the senior boys behind us, we could not help staring at the dozen or so un-uniformed boys leaning casually, almost lounging, against the walls on each side of the room. These, we gathered, were from the lower and upper sixth forms – and they were not boys but fully grown men. We could have easily mistaken them for young teachers. The browns and rusts and blues of their jackets and ties and suits stood out in stark contrast to our maroon blazers and grey trousers.

I knew well why I began to idolize Bob Wilson within days of that first meeting, when, as house captain, he welcomed us with a toothy smile, looking down at us, for he was tall and gangly. Bob was that being most hallowed in English school life culture: he was a natural all-rounder in every aspect of school life. He was living proof that Harry Wharton of the fictional Greyfriars School was not just a figment of Frank Richards's imagination; he refuted any belief I may have harboured that such perfect all-rounders do not exist in real life.

Yet it speaks poorly of us in the first form that we did not then find it strange that Bob Wilson would donate so much of his spare time to us. Rather too quickly, perhaps, we took our mentor's presence for granted. Such was our self-absorption and arrogance.

For the invisible, inquisitive observer, the answer to his question could not lie in the school's tradition or its social order, for not all sixth-formers were as driven as Bob. He could have done his bare duty as house captain and no one would have thought twice of it. So what made Bob Wilson tick?

Our observer would have quickly discovered why so many of us adored Bob: he was a Renaissance Man. Like most such persons his strength lay in being very good in almost everything he did without necessarily being the best in any one thing. As a scholar, there were others in the sixth form who were his superiors and yet he was held in such high regard by the masters that they felt he had more than a fair chance of winning a scholarship to Oxford. In football and cricket he represented the school, if not in the first elevens.

Bob Wilson had a twin brother named Bill, and once I had got over the shock of their resemblance, I managed to distinguish between them. In the beginning, whenever I saw one or the other, apart or together, I got into the habit of singing softly the signature song from the children's television programme, *Bill and Ben the Flower Pot Men* – 'Bill' and 'Ben' being, of course, twins. If this irritated Bob he never showed it. Later, I realized how annoying it must have been, how silly I must have sounded.

Bill Wilson belonged to another house, and so I never got to know him properly. They were both in the school choir, they acted together in one of the school plays we saw, and they both had roles in an operetta the school staged, called *Formula from Space*, composed by the senior music master, Mr Eade. But, it was Bob who had the edge on his twin. He had one of the lead roles in the operetta; and it was Bob who became school captain in my second year at Bemrose, and would stay on as school captain for another successive year. These were Bob Wilson's most obvious, visible accomplishments. He had yet another more subtle quality which perhaps we did not consciously realize: he was never condescending to the juniors; in modern jargon, he never talked down to us.

All this might tell our hypothetical observer why the boys liked Bob, but they did not answer the main question: what drove him?

Perhaps, the observer would conclude, that what motivated Bob Wilson was a masala of many traits. Perhaps he was an immensely kind and caring person, unusual for a person of his age; perhaps he felt some need to help the vulnerable – and we, in the first form, were certainly that; perhaps he possessed a yearning to be a leader, and mentoring twelve-year-olds was one expression of this desire; perhaps there was within him a hard streak of competitiveness which demanded that Newton House –

his house – must win all the inter-house competitions, and so he felt it his obligation to guide us to this end.

Whatever the cause, Bob Wilson took it upon himself to coach the Newton first-form football team, to train us for cross-country and to guide the cricket team. He was our choir master for the musical competition, in which we sang the hauntingly beautiful 'German Lullaby', a piece which, whenever I hear it (as I have done recently in a recording by Charlotte Church), conjures up an image of an empty classroom somewhere in Bemrose School at lunchtime, and rehearsals, and Bob in front waving a baton and mouthing the words. And he relished every success we achieved.

I established a rapport with Bob within days of that first Newton House meeting. I adopted him as my guru. As for Bob, perhaps my basic and visible foreignness made me the ultimate minority in Bemrose, for I was the only non-white boy in school. In his eyes, perhaps, I appeared to be especially vulnerable. Whatever be the reason, he took a special interest in my welfare. Was it my imagination that he was especially pleased whenever I scored a goal or ran well or – later, in the cricket season – had a good spell at the crease? And when, at the end of the first year, I did abysmally in my exams, he took time to draw me aside in the main corridor, just outside the masters' common room and console me, as I wondered what my parents would say.

Academics! It began well enough, I suppose. I must have done rather well in the 11-plus, for I was placed in the top of four sections in the first form. Each of the school's forms (the lordly sixth forms excepted, of course) were organized into four sections, L, M, G and S; L having the most academically superior students of the year, then M, and so on. (What these letters stood for I never learned; perhaps they were the start of some ponderous Latin words, but I simply took them arbitrarily to stand for Latin, Mathematics, Geography and Science.) I was placed in form 1L.

Thus I was among the brightest and the best. Perhaps this made me feel excessively cocky about my intellectual worth. The sad fact was that I went more or less off the academic rails in my first year in Bemrose.

Clearly, my initial enthrallment with the likes of Mr Bennett, the headmaster, Mr Norville, my housemaster, Mr Eade, the senior music master, Mr Smellie, my Latin master – who always carried with him an air of abstraction, as if he perpetually dwelt in that ancient land whose tongue we were learning in his class – did not suffice as inspiration. Perhaps it was just the idea of learning that gripped me rather than the practical matter of learning itself. In any case, in classroom matters, my first year in Bemrose School was a total haze. My mind was on everything but my studies.

I could not get enough of football and cricket and basketball and cross-country. If Bob Wilson was my personal guru, I had other lesser idols in the sixth forms: Galloway in basketball, Selby in track, Draper in swimming. As for the masters, I may have stood in awe of some of them, but it was the senior sports master, Danny Rees, whose approval I sought. I entered an oil painting I had done in the Hobbies Exhibition and it won first prize in the junior category. It brought glory to Newton House; what mattered to me was that, and that it had pleased Bob Wilson. More glory for the house when we won the inter-house, first-form football competition.

Nor had my New World life turned me away from the Old: I watched with immense satisfaction as Blackpool turned on the style. Jackie Mudie was scoring goals galore, and Matthews, at forty-two, was manifesting his magic as if age did not matter.

I did not abandon my bookishness, but it was not the textbooks that I perused. I haunted the school library whenever I could, but only to read detective stories and thrillers. The library had a small but growing paperback section and I had my first glimpse of Penguin Books. Agatha Christie filled my reading time, augmented by Ngaio Marsh, and occasional forays into Edgar Wallace and John Buchan. At last I was reading grown-up-ish stuff, with tantalizing hints of sex and seduction coyly tucked into the text. I did not know then the word 'subtext', but one of the excitements of those books was to uncover the sexual subtext for my titillation. Then there were the riches of the *Wisden Cricketers' Almanack*: without being disloyal to football, I rapidly brought my knowledge of cricketing history up to scratch. The feats of C. B. Fry and W. G. Grace, Victor Trumper and Harold Larwood, became as familiar to me, thanks to *Wisden*, as those of Steve Bloomer and Billy Meredith and Alex James and Dixie Dean in football. I had my first glimpse of the paradoxes of the British Raj as I learned of Prince Ranjitsinhji and Duleepsinhji and the Nawab of Pataudi – Indians who played for England.

Oddly enough, I read *Wisden* mostly over the winter months. Perhaps this was a manner of denial of the awfulness of winter days when I would cycle home at four o'clock in cold, wet darkness. Indeed, the very act of reading some of the match descriptions in *Wisden* would sometimes overwhelm me with a kind of longing for the summer days.

We were distracted by the New Music more than ever before. Elvis Presley had invaded the British Isles; in Graham's room, we heard 'Heartbreak Hotel' and 'Hound Dog', and 'Teddy Bear' again and again; we could not get enough of him. I learned by heart the lyrics of Frankie Lyman's 'I'm Not a Juvenile Delinquent', and Paul Anka's 'Diana'. In the changing room, as we donned our football strips, we hummed and whistled Tommy Steele's 'Singing the Blues'. My friend, Tony Moore, older and more precocious than the rest of us, smitten by one of his sister's friends, a girl called Marion, would sit on a low wooden fence at the top of Wheeldon Avenue and wait for her to pass by. And every time he would see her, he would sing the refrain from this song:

> *The moon and stars no longer shine*
> *The dream is gone I thought was mine*
> *There's nothing left for me to do but*
> *Cry-y-y-y over you*

– to her great discomfiture and our amusement.

Elvis came to town – to the cinema, in the movie *Loving You*. This posed a dilemma, however, for the second feature of the double billing was not for general showing. This meant that we could not enter the cinema without an adult as company.

In desperation, I followed a strategy some of the others had tried. I waited patiently outside the cinema; I would ask the adults going in whether I could accompany them – as if I were with them. They all declined and I was almost in despair till a solitary lady, she must have been in her late twenties or early thirties, smilingly took pity on me. Because of her, not only did I see my first Elvis Presley movie, but also a forbidden film, meant for 'restricted' or 'mature' viewing.

If I had been expecting some salacious excitement in the second feature I was sorely disappointed, and I wondered what all the fuss was about. There was much more of sexual dalliances around me in the auditorium than on the screen. The hall was chockfull of teenagers, sixteen- and seventeen-year-olds, couples, who between screams when Elvis did his wiggle and sang his songs, spent time groping and fumbling each other.

The whole school, it seemed, went beserk one time with the oddest of fashions – brilliant, garish, yellow and green and orange socks. We juniors would wear them outside school hours but

then some of the senior boys dared to wear them to school bring-
ing the wrath of the authorities on them. The craze vanished as
suddenly as it had begun.

I had, as they say, a full life, but the classroom had no place in
it – with one exception: despite my disaffection with academic
affairs that first year in Bemrose, I developed a deep love for
English literature. English was the one class I looked forward to –
especially when our teacher (whose face I can still see clearly in
my mind's eye but whose name escapes me) and we pupils read
aloud from Shakespeare. This was my first encounter with the
Bard.

I watched spellbound a staging of *Macbeth* as the school's
annual play, savouring the gothic menace, the passions, the play
of words. Decades later, I would see Orson Welles's film version,
and then Roman Polanski's very gory interpretation. Both times,
it was the stage in the Bemrose School Hall, viewed from the
gallery upstairs, that would rush to my inner eye. In Shakespeare,
I found at last a match for the magic of Stanley Matthews!

My English classes must have had an insidious but positive
effect on my overall literary standards for, at last, the classics
which my mother had so wanted me to read suddenly began to
make sense, and she watched with some satisfaction as I consumed rapidly *A Tale of Two Cities*, and Walter Scott – and then,
with Mark Twain and Harriet Beecher Stowe, and my mother's
copy of *Little Women*, a very different view of America than the
one I knew from movies and rock 'n' roll entered my consciousness.

It seemed that even my expectations of the detective stories
were raised: once I had discovered Arthur Conan Doyle and G. K.
Chesterton in the school library, Hercule Poirot and Miss Marple
and Inspector Alleyn became rather one-dimensional when
confronted with Sherlock Holmes and Father Brown – though I

must admit that something about the priest made me queasy. Perhaps the trauma of my encounter with Miss Sullivan and the catechism had left an indelible unease in my mind about all things Catholic.

Whether my newly acquired sensibility for English literature was the reason or not I cannot say, but I discovered something else from reading *Wisden*: that cricket writing had a poetry of its own, a cadence that was totally missing from the pieces I had pored over in my precious football books. The essays of Neville Cardus and John Arlott and R. C. Robertson-Glasgow were to the articles in *Charles Buchan's Football Annual* as the stories by Chesterton were to those by Edgar Wallace.

This disturbed me in an obscure way. Why was this? What was it about cricket that was missing in football that the writings on the two sports differed so drastically? Why was it that when I read John Arlott on cricket I felt like a grown-up, whereas reading John Thompson on football I felt I was a child?

Of course, I understood, but hazily, by way of an example. I realized that David Newman would no more read Cardus than he would read the *Manchester Guardian*. Only later would I articulate the place of class and education in the scheme of things: that cricket had its 'Gentlemen', the 'amateurs' whose surname on the batting list was always preceded by their initials – a C. B. Fry, a P. B. H. May, a D. S. Shepherd; they were the Cambridge and Oxford Blues. Amateurs had once played for professional football clubs but those days had long disappeared, and I could think of only two players of recent times – G. H. Robb of Tottenham Hotspurs, and W. Slater, once of Blackpool and then of Wolves – who played in the top league. Footballers emerged from the mines and the factories, they were once boys who went to work at fourteen or fifteen and came from families who lived on mean streets with outdoor toilets and no hot water.

And so, I decided, Neville Cardus wrote for his kind, and Charles Buchan for his kind. And they were poles apart in class and education.

Yet, one day many years later, I would sit in the Eden Gardens stadium in Calcutta and watch India play the touring English side. I would survey the massive throng of humanity around me. Hearing their insistent chant I would be reminded – not of Trent Bridge in Nottingham or the Oval in London – but of the Baseball Ground and Molineux in Wolverhampton. I realized then that the scene I was seeing, this crowd of 60–70-thousand strong, those people leaning out of every window of the All India Radio building behind the ground, this whole charged atmosphere – this was no different from the spectacle at English football grounds. This panorama before my eyes was as much tribalistic and ritualistic and primitive as any of the football matches I remembered seeing. Perhaps, I thought, as I lit a cigarette, the ethos of English cricket was quite different from the ethos of Indian cricket. Perhaps cricket in India affords the same emotional – the same viscerally emotional – appeal that football does in England; perhaps despite the Maharajahs and the Nawabs, cricket in India was as much a game of the 'masses', as much a street game, a game diffused into the very texture of the Indian mass psyche as football was in England.

The outcome of that frenetic first Bemrose year was, in hindsight, predictable. At the end of the summer term I was placed almost bottom of the class. I learned I would be moved to Form 2M in the coming school year. In footballing terms I had been relegated from L (First Division) to M (Second Division)!

I was stunned. Bob Wilson's attempts to console me may have helped somewhat, but I could only think of my parents' shame. I watched them with dread as they read the year-end school report – and the verdict scrawled by my form teacher and approved by the headmaster. My parents could not have liked what they read, but they did not quite comprehend the implications of the transfer from 'L' to 'M'. They consulted my former tutor, Joyce, and as she explained, I could only look on miserably at their dismay, their disbelieving faces, as if the bottom had fallen out of their world.

As Bob Wilson had consoled me, so Joyce tried to soothe them. She said it was not the end of the world; she said I had ample time to make up, and return to the top section, well before I had to take my O levels.

My parents – my mother especially – possessed an immeasurable quantity of optimism that came in very handy in these troubled times. Mollified by Joyce's words, they recovered soon enough. As for me, I had all the resilience of a twelve-year-old. I recovered my aplomb; I also took heart with Joyce's words. After all, Derby County had just won promotion from the Third Division (North) back into the Second Division. If the Rams could do it, so could I.

13

A Cousin from India

That year involved changes at Home as significant as those Away. Our longest and closest family friend in Derby among the Bengali bachelors, Mihir Sen – Mihir-*da* to me – left for India. His training at International Combustion had ended, and he went to take a position in the same firm in Calcutta. We would miss him terribly – his rumbunctiousness, his self-deprecating, wry stories about adventures in the pursuit of women (which I could only glean by straining my ears while pretending to read a book in our sitting room), his excitability. In my case, Mihir-*da* was much in my mind the following summer when the West Indian cricketers arrived in England, their first visit since the famous 1950 tour; as that time, in this squad there were the Three Ws, Worrall, Weekes and Walcott, and the spinmen, Ramadhin and Valentine, and throughout the summer I would hear inside my head Mihir-*da*'s voice singing the calypso I had learned from him – and the refrain would reverberate in my ear, 'With those little pals of mine / Ramadhin and Valentine'.

This departure was counterpointed by an arrival which would have a profound effect on me. My cousin Biman came to Derby

all the way from Calcutta. Like all the cousins younger than him
in our joint family home, I knew him as Moni-*da* – though obviously I had not addressed him so in years. Indeed, all I
remembered about him was his name and what we called him.

Moni-*da* was ten years older than me – hence the '-*da*'. He was
a civil engineer, and my father had helped in securing him a position in a local company called F. C. Construction, a name which
would become as familiar to us as Derbyshire Royal Infirmary.
And just as I had picked up medical terms from my father – terms
I little understood, like 'tympanoplasty operation' and 'septum'
and 'cochlea' – so also, within a few months, I had acquired (with
as little understanding) a miniscule civil engineering vocabulary –
'reinforced concrete' and 'retaining walls' and 'prestressed concrete' and 'soil mechanics'.

When Moni-*da* first arrived on a dismal, wet November afternoon, we looked at each other warily. In my case, it had been so
long since I had seen my cousins in Calcutta that they had almost
become figures in some distant land of myths and legends in
my memory. There was an element of unreality in seeing one of
these figures before my very eyes. It was quite overwhelming. In
Moni-*da*'s case, I suppose he was uncertain about how I would
respond to him; perhaps he was under the apprehension that I
was some totally Anglicized brat who had no interest in his
family back in India.

Within a few days, our wariness had melted away. Perhaps he
was relieved that I was not as brattish as he had feared. I even
managed a bit of the Bengali language. In turn, I was enchanted
with the idea of a brother – which is what cousins raised in joint
families in India thought they were.

As an only child I was never allowed to forget that I was an
only child – not by my parents but others. I once heard my father
say that Bengalis could be as brutal to each other as children

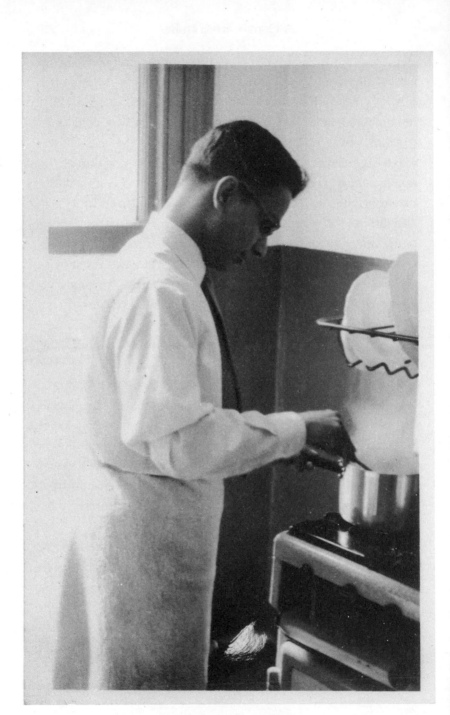

My cousin Biman, in Derby.

could be cruel to their peers – especially when it came to things like complexion or the colour of one's skin or looks. I knew what he meant. I would often overhear the people sitting in our living room making the most horrible remarks about others. It was shocking to hear the callousness with which someone would say about someone else, 'she's so ugly!' or 'he's so dark!'

I knew what my father meant, for on many occasions an adult, on meeting me for the first time, would exclaim, 'What a pity you're an only child!' – as if it was some terrible disease, like leprosy. This would be inevitably followed by a question which, as inevitably, would infuriate me, 'Whom do you love the most, your father or your mother?' I never understood why they would ask me this – unless it was an attempt to embarrass me or to invoke from me a response that would humiliate one of my parents. Fortunately, I had developed quite early the proper defence mechanism against this: I would simply look away.

Many years later, my mother told me that each time she heard someone make a remark about me as an only child, she would be consumed with guilt. She said that as long as we were in India, within the compass of a joint family, lost in a crowd of cousins, it did not matter. But after we came to England, she would watch painfully, in Nottingham, in particular, as I played make-believe games by myself on winter weekend afternoons, Cowboys and Red Indians, or Robin Hood and Little John, games that involved two people, two sides. She said that she would observe me taking turns at being one person then the other, talking aloud in two voices, and she would laugh aloud but she would be in tears inside.

I had comforted her then, and told her that if she had ever talked to me about it, she would have felt quite unburdened. I told her that being an 'only child' had never bothered me a bit. I suppose I had accepted it as a fact of life very early on, and never gave it much thought. And when someone made a silly remark about it, I ignored it completely. She asked me – did I not ever feel lonely? I gave her the most honest answer I could: I had so many interests that kept me busy, that I never had the time to feel lonely. I told her that when all else failed, I had my books. I reminded her I was always bookish.

Yet, I must admit that having Moni-*da* around the flat made me feel warm in a way that was quite different from, say, having Mihir-*da* around the flat. It felt brotherly rather than friendly! He brought with him a strong whiff of India, of Bengal, of Calcutta, of our family home in north Calcutta. In fact, he imported another New World altogether into the Home. He also brought new friends into our lives, somewhat different from the Bengalis that we had come to know in Nottingham and Derby. They were better educated: they held university degrees in engineering and they were also more literate in a wider sense of the word. Even I could sense this trait. From them, I learned about the Bengal Engineering College, where they had studied, which, Moni-*da* told me with manifest pride, had celebrated its centenary the year before, which Jawaharlal Nehru, India's prime minister, had attended; he told me with a tinge of awe in his voice about a place in America called the MIT, the world's greatest engineering school, he said.

Some of Moni-*da*'s classmates visited us from London where they were postgraduate students at Imperial College; when they were around, they would talk about the diplomas they aspired towards, and I was soon familiar with enigmatic initials, DIC, and AMIStructE – letters they were hoping to attach behind their names.

It was because of all these excited discussions that for a while I developed an intense and quite useless fascination with abbreviations of degrees and diplomas and institutions. I would open my father's *Concise Oxford English Dictionary* and look up all the abbreviations listed in a front section. I became something of an expert in knowing what FRCS, and AMIMechE, and FIM, and FRS, and FInstFuel, and the like stood for.

I taught Moni-*da* the nuances of English football. He assumed Mihir-*da*'s mantle in educating me about Indian sports, not just cricket but hockey for which India was then famous. I heard the name of Dhyan Chand, who, he said, was to hockey what Matthews was to football and Bradman to cricket.

Moni-*da* had digs on White Street, just off Kedleston Road, a few hundred yards from us. Of course, he took all his meals with us. Very quickly, my evenings would be ruined if for some reason he did not turn up when expected.

14

A Girl Like Me

Perhaps tired of the English seaside, my parents opted to spend the summer holidays in the British capital.

I had visited London only once, since moving to Nottingham, after our first year in England. I had accompanied my father who had a medical meeting to attend in London. We stayed in a small hotel – where I cannot remember. What remained in my memory was that one morning I was left alone while my father went to the meeting, and I spent the whole morning outside the hotel, talking to a bunch of boys who were all West Ham United supporters. For some reason we became embroiled in a footballing argument. Fortunately, nothing sinister came of it, thanks to my knowledge of football history – apparently I impressed them hugely, and we parted on amicable terms.

My father's interest in animals – dead or alive – was unbounded. Mercifully, we did not visit Regent's Park Zoo, but I could not avoid an afternoon in the Natural History Museum where, after showing me the massive cross section of a centuries-old tree with its annual rings clearly marked out, my father stood, far more spellbound than I, gazing up at the gigantic blue whale suspended from the ceiling of a long hall.

That was some time ago, so I looked forward to this holiday with much excitement. I was, after all, visiting the homeland of Arsenal and Chelsea and Tottenham Hotspur football clubs, of Lord's and the Oval.

We stayed with an old friend of my father, Dr Prasun Choudhury and his family. They lived in a house – and this was my first awareness of an Indian, a Bengali at that, occupying an entire house in England, in the manner of my English friends. In all the schools I had attended, I was something of an enigma to some of my friends, because I lived in a flat. One classmate in Bemrose, well-meaning and friendly otherwise, gazed at me wide-eyed as if I were an interesting biological specimen when I told him that I lived in a flat. He said he had never before met such a person. He said he could not imagine what it was like to live in a flat. Defensively, I said it was not that unusual – but he was not convinced.

In fact, in England, I had never lived any other way, and since all our Bengali acquaintances, temporary residents that they were in this country, all lived, not even in flats, but digs, I may have assumed that Indians who came to this country lived in the way we all did. It was a massive revelation to learn otherwise, and I wondered why we did not have a house of our own in Derby.

But that week in London, all else paled into insignificance the evening we went to Dr and Mrs Biswas's house for dinner. (They too owned a house, I noted parenthetically.) Dr Biswas was a general practitioner, as far as I recall; whether my father knew him from Calcutta I do not remember. But his wife, Rekha – I called her Rekha-*mashi*, Aunt Rekha – was an old schoolfriend of my mother, and they hadn't seen each other for a long time. London was only a few hours by train from Derby, and why we had not visited the capital more often, why the two friends had not met for years, were puzzles I never did resolve. After all, football supporters travelled by train all over the country to watch their teams' away games.

That evening, at the Biswases', I met a girl. Her name was Kumkum, she was their younger daughter, and exactly my age; she had an older sister named Krishna, and we took to one another within minutes. The fact that both the sisters were extremely vivacious, and Kumkum was rather pretty, made it all the easier for me.

I was not especially shy of girls. My primarily boys' world was peppered with the odd girl or two. I was quite friendly with several in our neighbourhood – in particular, Susan Scattergood, the butcher's daughter, right across Kedleston Road from us, for whom I had a special affection for teaching me to ride a bike; the Heldrich sisters, Avis and Janice, next door, whom I had known since first coming to Derby; and Pat Moore, who became a good friend in my later years. Then there were Pat's friends from Parkfield Cedars School who occasionally joined us. But they were just that – friends. Except for Pat's brother, Tony, older and more precocious than us, none of us was 'into girls' – yet.

That evening, I tasted the delights of flirting for the first time. It was all very platonic, of course, but nevertheless charged with the promise of possibilities. It was all talk, banter, a great deal of laughter and verbal sparring, the occasional cuss word to demonstrate to one another how worldly we were. For once, I did not utter a word about football or cricket. We explored each others' taste in music. We compared notes – on the Everly Brothers, Buddy Holly, Elvis (of course) and the exciting voice of Paul Anka, only a few years older than us, who had just burst onto the pop scene, belting out 'Diana'.

While the adults chattered in the living room, we were left

undisturbed in another part of the house. The two sisters put on a record and taught me to 'jive'. They introduced me to an Indian game called 'karram' which reminded me a bit of snooker, except that it was played on a polished, wooden, square board with pockets only at the four corners, with small, flat, smooth, wooden disks the size of a penny instead of balls, that were hit with the back of one's fingers rather than with cues. I had the vaguest memory of watching my older cousins playing the game in Calcutta.

I had not forgotten the Bengali language. I could even read it, haltingly and often with comical results. Indeed, when my parents and their Bengali intimates were in want of amusement, my mother would ask me to read aloud from a well-known Bengali children's book, and they would collapse in laughter at my mispronunciations. For some reason, their hilarity at my cost never offended me. Kumkum and Krishna could also speak Bengali, perhaps better than I did. That evening, I had the most unusual experience of speaking to someone of my age in the kind of hotchpotch mix of English and Bengali the adults usually spoke, except that we spoke more in English than in Bengali. Still, I was surprised with myself, with my inclination to speak Bengali at all. I had never done this since coming to England – I had never known boys or girls of my age who knew Bengali.

At night, lying in bed, I could hardly sleep. I kept replaying our exchanges, Kumkum's and mine. I kept hearing her voice, her laughter. I conjured up the image of her face. I was smitten with her. I was not yet thirteen!

Our hosts had a collection of records, all 78 rpms which I would browse through. They were mostly Bengali songs which, at that particular time, did not interest me. There were, however, a handful of English records and among them was one by an old favourite of mine before the coming of rock 'n' roll – Ruby

Murray. The song was called 'It's the Irish in Me'. Her wistful voice which I had once loved and that particular song seemed to match exactly my mood at the moment, and I played the record again and again, whenever we were indoors, no doubt to the adults' perplexity.

I met Kumkum and her sister once more when they all came to our hosts', the Choudhurys, to dinner. We exchanged greetings as if we had known each other for ever. I did not want the evening to end. When they left, Kumkum and I promised to write to each other. We never did, of course.

I have never heard that particular Ruby Murray song again, though I have a whole collection of her recordings. But the yearning woven into that particular song, and the first two or three lines of the lyrics have remained, and that song is inextricably interwoven in my head with the magic of those two evenings.

Of course, we did other things that week. One morning, my parents and I took the tube to Earls Court and walked along the Warwick Road to number 23, our first abode in England. We stared up at the second-floor window where I would wait impatiently each evening to spot my father walking home from the hospital. I turned around to look, with detached interest, at the school exactly opposite the house, St Matthias. This was my first English school, where I had learned the language, where I had learned that India was in a place called Asia, where I had almost burst into tears on hearing 'Greensleeves' for the first time in music class, where I had my first experience of being called 'brownie' and 'Injun'.

We made the inevitable trek to the Natural History Museum where my mother and I waited phlegmatically as my father gazed once more at the blue whale. He claimed that this was a real whale, but I was not convinced.

Of course, we visited Madame Tussaud's. My father just had

to see the image of the Sleeping Beauty once again; the crafts-man in him could only admire the illusion of a living, sleeping girl. We looked at the images of Nehru and Gandhi, both of which left my parents indignant – for making Nehru too dark, my mother complained, and not at all like him; for making Gandhi look too wizened, too naked, my father said.

On the penultimate day of our vacation, I took the tube with some Bengali bachelors to the Oval, to watch the final test between England and the West Indies, at which Tom Graveney, scored a century and a half.

For several days after we returned to Derby – which seemed unbelievably tepid after London – I went through a strange period. I had always been restless whenever we came back from a holiday, but I would be back to my usual self in a day or two. This time it was different. For three or four days, I hardly left the house. Friends – Alan and Johnny and Graham and Robin Darbyshire, in ones, two or threes would ring the door bell, I would poke my head out of the living-room window, exchange a few words, hesitate, and then make some excuse. I did not want to be with them.

I could not understand myself. On the train journey home I had mentally rubbed my hands in anticipation of the stories I would tell my friends – about the test match, about the Tower of London, about the girl I had met. But when the time came, I said nothing, I retreated into myself like the tortoise I had had in Nottingham, which would withdraw its head into its shell at will.

If my parents noticed that I was more or less mooning around the flat all day long for two or three days in succession, if they noticed this aberrant behaviour on my part, they said nothing. They may have noticed my unusual animation in London, and they may have wondered at this drastic change of mood, but they made no comment to me.

I realized what 'having the blues' meant. I would hear, in my head, Tommy Steele's 'Singing the Blues', and it matched my mood well.

Eventually, of course, I shook off my ennui and resumed normal service. At some point in time, however, I realized the true reason for that peculiar and unwonted phase I went through. It was the fact that this girl, Kumkum Biswas, was a girl like me. In fact, she (and her sister) were the first persons I had met in England who belonged exactly to my world. Every one else I knew was either Indian or English. So far, I had considered myself to be the only person I knew who was Indian and English, whose world was a kind of amalgam, a masala of both Indianness and Englishness – till I met Kumkum and her sister. They, too, were of this same world. That was why we had been so comfortable with one another – why (in the jargon of a later age) we 'bonded' together so rapidly. I realized then that my temporary disaffection with my friends was because they did not belong to this world – they would not understand what it was to belong to this world. For those few days, they became alien to me.

I would meet Kumkum only once more – in London again the next year; and as before, we talked like very old friends. But then, my life was turned drastically around and we never saw each other again, though every now and then I would overhear my mother speak of Rekha-*mashi*. Years later, I saw Satyajit Ray's Bengali film, *Teen Kanya* (Three Daughters}, in which one of the main characters was played by an actress named Kanika Majumdar. My mother said that she was Rekha-*mashi*'s sister. I thought briefly then of Kumkum and her sister. I may have asked my mother where they were, what they were doing. I have forgotten her reply. Only Ruby Murray's voice and the words and the tune of 'It's the Irish in Me' remained as a memento of that brief encounter.

15

Clouds Heap upon Clouds

In the weeks just after my thirteenth birthday I began to hear snatches of conversation that vaguely disturbed me.

I had often heard my parents talk of leaving England, of 'going back home'. In fact, this was a staple topic of conversation whenever the Bengali crowd gathered together. It was certainly the bachelors' fantasy. I knew from listening in on their chatter that from the day they set foot on England, they began to 'save' – to put away a shilling here, half-a-crown there – for that day when, training or apprenticeship or higher studies done, and no further reason to linger on, they would pack their belongings, things brought from home, new things bought in England – perhaps a Rolleiflex camera, a tailored suit or two, a tweed jacket from John Burton, shirts from Marks & Spencer, and odds and ends for mothers and sisters – and depart for Southampton or Tilbury to catch the next available P&O ship back home.

I had seen several of them leave this way. I had observed, numbly and almost in tears, Mihir-*da*'s departure. And I had listened idly to my parents' wistful talk. But I never paid much attention to them, for I felt that we were like a seaport, solid, fixed, and these others, some of whose names and faces were already blurred in my memory, were like ships that stopped for a while and then moved on.

But these days, the tone was different; there was a sober, sharper, more focused edge to it. Perhaps their more recent talk of 'going back home' was a reflection of the general ambience that seemed to have gathered momentum – of farewells and departures. My cousin Moni-*da*'s arrival and his daily presence may have consoled them but it was not enough. There were other factors, other influences, some large, some small.

For one thing, there was my mother's homesickness, her deeply ingrained sense of loneliness and isolation. I had come to understand, as the years had passed, that she had never come to terms with the Western idea of a family composed just of husband, wife and children living apart from, and independent of, aunts and uncles and cousins and grandparents. From the day our ship berthed in Liverpool that grey morning, she had felt trapped, because she was so utterly severed from the boisterous, exuberant, densely peopled, event-rich life she had known before and after marriage. Each wedding of a cousin she could not attend, each birth of a nephew or niece she could not witness, each episode in the endless cycle of births, birthdays, marriages, anniversaries, *pujas*, *holi* (the spring festival), celebrations of any kind – each such event that passed her by that she could not witness but only imagine from letters from home, helped drive the spike of loneliness still deeper into her soul.

Later, I realized that she probably suffered from these absences more than she did the eclipse of her singing career. She certainly regretted that: she would like to have gone on with her recordings and performances at concerts and sessions in the studios of All India Radio, but she sang because she liked to, it was a part of her being; the professionalism and the careerism were secondary.

In England, by odd connections, she had some opportunities to
do these things. Once, we travelled to Manchester where she sang
on stage to an Indian gathering; and in fact, in addition, the three
of us, my parents and I sang together a popular English/
American song, 'Oh My Papa', that same evening. Another time
she went to Birmingham to perform, perhaps on the occasion of
India's Independence Day. And when the BBC Overseas Service
decided to set up a Bengali programme – they named it *Vichitra*,
meaning 'diversity' or 'variety' – they chose my mother to record
the signature piece for the programme, an immensely patriotic
composition by Atul Prasad Sen, a distinguished Bengali poet and
composer. The song, written well before independence, urged
every one to proclaim that India would once more resume her
rightful and pre-eminent place in the assembly of nations.
Whenever in later years I heard this song, I would see in my
mind's eye my mother rehearsing in our living room, with a man
from London, named Mukul Das, accompanying her on the
piano accordion.

Yet, there was no doubt – if she had to choose between staying
in England and enjoying, in some magical fashion, her musical
career, and giving it all up but being back in Calcutta amongst her
people – she would willingly have chosen the latter.

She was not the type to mope, however. She led an active
social life; she had several close English women friends who often
dropped by for tea and talk. Joyce was one, but there were others
including Frieda Sturgess, whose father was a city alderman and
evidently of some local stature for the secondary modern school
down the road was named after him. My mother was involved in
charity work, in the Women's Voluntary Service, and through the
WVS she met other ladies of local prominence. One was connected in some way with someone high up in the *Derby Evening
Telegraph*, and she arranged a memorable visit for Graham Dean

and me to the *Telegraph* press to watch the making of a newspaper. The highlight of that visit was a memento given to each of us, a glossy, ten-by-eight photo of the current Derby County team.

But all this could not erase her yearning for 'home'. Nor did the many visits by relatives from India help – indeed, if anything their departures made things worse. They included several aunts and uncles of hers (my grandaunts and granduncles) and her cousins, both the unmarried ones and those with their spouses. She adored them all, they adored her, and when they were gone she was inconsolable for days.

The best and worst of these times happened about the time we moved from Nottingham to Derby, when my maternal uncle, her only brother, and his new bride came to stay with us for a few days. They were on an extended (and belated) European honeymoon. I worshipped my debonair uncle whom I called *Mamu*, for he had spoiled me silly from the day I was born. This time, though, he was upstaged in my view by my new aunt, whom I called *Mimi*. She entranced me with her very un-Bengali grey eyes, pert nose and dimpled smile. We got along famously. Inevitably, the time came for them to leave, and this time I was as desolate as my mother.

I could always make out when she was going through a bout of homesickness: it did not matter where she was in the flat, or what she was doing, cooking or knitting or sitting by the window; I knew she was in that mood for she would almost always sing one of Tagore's slower, sadder songs. Two were her favourites when she was in that mood. One began (translated into English) 'Who wants to live in this foreign land?' The other was the one she sang most often, and it started with the words 'Clouds heap upon clouds'. To me, this song more than any other became the emblem of her longing for India.

My mother (back, right) with her English friends.

Strangely enough, I never saw tears in my mother's eyes when she was actually singing. It was as if this very act diverted her mind from her emotions. Years later, when I read Freud and learned about defence mechanisms, I realized that for my mother, her songs and her singing served as a kind of defence mechanism. They warded off the low spirits which would otherwise overwhelm her.

The effect on her listeners, though, was just the opposite. There was one particular evening in our flat, amid a large gathering of our Indian friends, mostly Bengalis as usual, perhaps it was on the occasion of India's Independence Day or Republic Day, I cannot recall. My mother was at her harmonium and singing patriotic songs. And I would see tears streaming down the cheeks of the menfolk, who otherwise were brash, loud, blustering, perpetually teasing one another. These were tears of homesickness. Bengalis are hopelessly sentimental; and music and the songs of Tagore and D. L. Roy and Kazi Nazrul Islam, household names in the pantheon of Bengali poets, make them weepy – even the men.

Then there was the strained atmosphere inside our house. For the most part there was a kind of stillness. The Howells had left some time ago, though where they had gone I did not know. For a time before the attic bedsitter was re-occupied, my friends and I would venture into it to gaze out of the window at the street below, and generally enjoy its emptiness. One day we found a bunch of papers tucked away in one of the cupboards. They were love letters written by Mr Howell to Mrs Howell before they were married, when he was away, probably doing his National Service.

We had never read love letters before. The four of us, Graham, Johnny, Alan and I poured curiously and excitedly over them, seeking no doubt some erotic charge from their contents. We were loath to leave them behind – after all, we reasoned, they were no use to anyone else, and the Howells had obviously forgotten about them. So we hid them inside the thick hedge in Graham's back garden; every now and then, bored with other pastimes and seeking a bit of titillation, we would bring them out furtively, making sure Graham's parents were not around and read them aloud to one another.

Eventually, the attic flat was rented out, to a thin, taciturn, almost sullen, single woman who made no attempt to befriend us. This in itself was a new experience for me, for in every house we had lived, in London, then Nottingham, then Derby, the adults had always taken to me. Often, as with the Thomases in Nottingham, I was more their friend than my parents were.

This lady was clearly not that type! I would hear her pad up the staircase in the evening, past our flat, returning from wherever she worked. No stentorian, cheerful, tenor voice to break the afternoon lull with 'The Man from Laramie', and announce the advent of evening. Not even the hint of a hum.

Some years later, in Calcutta, my parents suddenly received an airmail letter from the Howells. The writer was Mrs Howell. She explained that they had extracted our Calcutta address from my father's bank in Derby – Grindlays or Westminster – where he still maintained an account. Privacy acts did not prevail in those simpler times.

They seemed to appeal to my parents for a forgiveness of sorts – for all the sad things, the bad things, that had happened at the end, they wrote – and recalled wistfully happier times. They still had no children, but they kept hoping, they said. They expressed a wish to visit India one day, and meet us again. In the meantime, they would like to keep in touch.

It was a long, dense letter, full of contrition, nostalgia, sadness, regrets for a friendship gone awry. They asked about me. My mother, excited, sentimental, replied almost immediately and I think a letter or two were exchanged. Inevitably, when all that could be said had been said, the letters tapered off.

The Amoses had also become rather quiet. Their son, Bob, still lived with them, and I would see him out walking arm-in-arm with the girl he was courting. I scarcely saw Pauline any more. I was still invited downstairs to watch the odd sporting event or a film on their television. It was on one such occasion, in February, that I sat with Mr Amos and watched, in disbelief, newsreel footage and stills of the scene of carnage, as the players of Manchester United, almost the whole team, died amid the snow and shattered metal pieces of a plane on the tarmac of Munich Airport. A few days later, I was there again to hear the news that Duncan Edwards had also passed away in hospital. We watched together footage of his games playing for Manchester United and for England, and listened numbly to the pundits paying homage to a player they thought was the most exciting footballer to emerge in Britain in the 1950s. Was it my imagination or did I detect tears in Mr Amos's eyes?

Bur the shadow over their relationship with my parents had been cast for too long and could never be dispelled. My parents felt simply too uncomfortable in that house; they felt unwelcome.

I was also vaguely aware of something amiss with my father's work. They never talked about it openly in my presence, but by picking up bits and pieces of their conversations with Moni-*da* I pieced together a kind of picture.

My father was bitterly disappointed in being passed over for a senior position that had opened up at the hospital. He felt that this failure was not because he was unqualified or undeserving, quite the contrary. He felt he had not got the job because he was not white. I had never seen my father so despondent – or at least despondent for such a long time. For a period, I found it difficult to stay at home on weekends or in the evenings after school; there was so much gloom around the flat.

Some time before Christmas, urged by Moni-*da* to 'move with the times', my parents bought a Bush electric record player. This was yet another portent of change, one that I viewed with mixed emotions. On the one hand, I could now buy records I had only handled wistfully in Dixons: LPs and EPs. On the other hand, with a great deal of sadness I put away our mechanical, wind-up gramophone, my uncle's going-away present to me when we left India. Its thick, metal-shiny playing arm which held the needle, curled up like a contented kitten, looked clumsy and prehistoric, compared to the lightweight 'pick-up' arm on the new player. The two devices bore no resemblance to each other, though they performed the same task. Even the names had changed – this new device was no longer a 'gramophone' but a 'record player'; it did not use 'needles' that had to be replaced after every third or fourth use but a 'stylus' which lasted for ages. Even the logo of His Master's Voice, the small rectangular picture of the dog staring expectantly at the horn sticking out of the phonograph (an even older, obsolete word), the very symbol of what we expected of a gramophone, was missing from the record player.

My mother's words mirrored my thoughts, when she said that there was a kind of solidity, a permanence to the gramophone which was absent from the new machine, despite its streamlined, plastic sleekness.

For all the years we had lived in England, Mamu's gift had been my precious companion even before I knew how to operate it. I had heard my first Tagore songs on it, before I knew who Tagore was and who the singer was. Its original green cover had been replaced once by red-coloured rexin, but otherwise it was as good as it had been when I bought my first two records in Nottingham, Tex Ritter's 'Do Not Forsake Me, Oh My

Darling' from the movie *High Noon*, and Doris Day's 'Secret Love' from *Calamity Jane*. My one consolation was that my father found a 'good home' for it : he gave it away to the chauffeur of the car which sometimes drove him to the infirmary for late-night or emergency calls. It was the chauffeur's gift to his small son.

. I mourned its passing, but not for long. Perhaps Moni-*da*'s practical outlook helped: this was progress, he said to me impatiently. Indeed! Very soon, all of a sudden, I was eschewing the familiar, eminently breakable 78s for the 33s and 45s. For Christmas, one of our Bengali friends, a civil engineer like Moni-*da* and from the same Alma Mater, presented me with an LP of the *Nutcracker Suite*. This was my first classical record, and I was surprised how much I liked it, especially the 'Waltz of the Flowers', which made me ache inside in a way I could never describe. Every time I listened to it, I imagined looking down from a balcony at some splendid scene in the hall below, with couples in eighteenth-century costumes whirling round and round.

Then one day, one of Moni-*da*'s friends brought with him from London an LP my father had wanted. He had bought it at the HMV Shop, and it was a recording by someone I had never heard of, a man called Ali Akbar Khan.

My mother explained that this, too, was classical music but from India. The instrument shown on the glossy album cover was a *sarod*, she said.

I have never seen my parents so excited. They said that this was a milestone in musical history, for this was the first Western recording of Indian classical music. That was why, they explained, it had an introduction by Yehudi Menuhin.

My mother tried to explain the idea of *ragas* and the nature of Indian classical music, and how it differed from European classical music. She described how *ragas* were associated with different moods and times of day and seasons. She told me that one side of the Ali Akbar Khan album was a performance of a morning *raga*, the flip side an evening one.

At first I was not particularly caught up in their excitement. But then, one Sunday morning I was woken just as dawn was breaking by the faintly muffled sound of the *sarod* – the morning *raga*, called *Sind Bhairavi*. Half asleep, I realized that the sound was coming from my parents' bedroom next door.

Later, when fully awake and brushing my teeth, I felt I had just emerged from a trance in which Yehudi Menuhin's voice, the rhythm of the *tabla*, the drums, the drone of the *tanpura* in the background, and the rich, deep sound of the *sarod* had formed one whole. I thought that I had been listening to the sound of an express train pounding along a rhythmic track as the *sarod* and the *tabla* reached their final, furious crescendo.

I found it strange and somehow wonderful how totally different these two types of classical music were – Tchaikovsky's *Nutcracker* and Ali Akbar Khan's *Sind Bhairavi*.

Perhaps what astonished me most was the effect of this album on my father. He loved music, but I had no idea that he loved Indian classical music so much. Listening to this album seemed to make him realize how much he had missed it all these years, for I do not recall we had any 78s with this kind of music. That album by Ali Akbar Khan was a kind of wake-up call, to tell him what his wife had been saying all along: there were things back home that he treasured, that they were missing out on, and that he, too, harboured yearnings for his homeland.

Despite these ominous signs, I went about enjoying my second year in Bemrose. There were new classmates for me, since my 'relegation' to Form 2M but I knew many of them already; for a few days I felt uncomfortable, but Joyce's words to my parents remained in my mind, and soon I managed to shake off my very wounded pride. I began to pay far more attention to classwork than before.

There were other major changes in school. Mr Bennett, the headmaster, had left at the end of the last summer term to take up a position in Bournemouth; there had been a sentimental farewell, and now we had a new headmaster, Dr W. R. C. Chapman. I felt immensely contented, for at last we had a 'Doctor' as head, much as the fictional Greyfriars School had a Doctor Locke and Tom Brown's Rugby School a Doctor Arnold as heads. My picture of what Bemrose Grammar School should be was complete!

We of Newton House were overjoyed when we learned that Bob Wilson was the new school captain. There was not a prouder boy in the whole of Derby than me! More than ever before, I saw him as my personal guru. The downside was that we saw less of him, but he was still our house captain, and he still mentored us to some extent.

Then a ripple of excitement ran through Newton House when we heard a new sixth-former had joined and was placed in our house. His name was Colin Oldham and – this was the important point – he was a very fine cricketer.

I found Colin Oldham fascinating. Tall and lanky, he wore an air of insouciance that I found irresistible, added to which was a hint of a drawl. For some reason, he came to know me a bit – as well as a sixth-former can know a second-former. He came to know me better by way of a curious incident.

I was walking to Bemrose one morning along Mackworth Road, past the Rec – why I was not biking that day, I cannot recall – when an older girl in the uniform of Parkfield Cedars School, passing by, stopped suddenly to talk to me. Did I know Colin Oldham? she asked. She had recognized my Bemrose blazer. I nodded. Could I deliver a letter to him? Surprised and then amused, I nodded.

If I wore a knowing smirk on my face when handing the letter over to Colin after morning assembly, he ignored it. But I noticed that he was perceptibly more warmly disposed towards me from then on, whether out of the kindness of his heart or because he thought I might tell all about this incident, I had no way of knowing.

At home, I began to notice an unusual influx of envelopes bearing Indian stamps, and also stamps from Malaya, even an African nation or two. My stamp collector's acquisitive instinct was still alive, and I grabbed the envelopes as soon as I could. But I also began to realize with inward dismay that my father was seriously exploring work possibilities in India and other countries. They did not confide in me, however, and I could not bring myself to speak to them about the unspeakable. Perhaps in my subconscious I believed that if we did not actually talk about this, the problem would go away.

Some time in late January, as we sat down for breakfast – it must have been a Sunday, for that was the only day in the week that the four of us, Moni-*da* included, ate breakfast together – my parents informed me that we were returning to India. We would be leaving in March, my father said.

I am not sure which stunned me more – the fact that we were leaving England or the fact that we would leave so soon. I have no recollection of what I said, or whether I said anything at all. What remains in my memory is the intensity of my misery, an emotion that returns whenever I recall that day.

What else did they say to me that morning? What explanation did they give as to why we would leave before the school year was finished? How did they console me? I remember nothing. What I do recall with complete clarity is that I put on my mackintosh, went downstairs, wheeled out my bike and rode into Markeaton Park. And I recall that it was a cold, grey, damp morning.

For several days I said nothing to my friends about all this. In school I avoided company as much as I could. At lunch break, after the meal, instead of joining the usual knockabout football on the field or the strange games we played in the cemented area in the front of the school building, I would disappear into the library and take refuge amidst the shelves; or I took solitary walks around the perimeter of the grounds, along the farthest side of the playing fields. That area was usually deserted at that time except for the occasional lonely runner out on a self-imposed training schedule.

At home, preparations commenced for our departure. Schedules of dates for ships leaving in March for Bombay arrived from the P&O Company, along with glossy brochures on ocean liners. My father, the maker of model galleons and ships, who still yearned to be a ship's surgeon, pored greedily over them. Suitcases were bought. Packing boxes appeared, from where I did not know. The process of uprooting our English life had begun. Suitcases, trunks and boxes were packed, unpacked and repacked. New items were bought: crockery, Derby Crown china, silverware, tablecloths of Nottingham lace, bedsheets, eiderdowns and bedcovers. My parents debated whether to buy a refrigerator and an electric cooking 'range', but after much discussion, they decided not to, because of the high customs duty they would have to pay in Bombay, for these were 'luxury' items, and, furthermore, Moni-*da* and a few of our Indian friends assured them that these items were being manufactured in India.

Presents: watches for my older cousins, handbags and shoes of assorted sizes for aunts and female cousins, walkie-talkie dolls that closed their eyes when horizontal and made wailing noises when upright for tots, new cousins of mine whom we would see for the first time. I listened to their animated talk and looked on with a kind of disbelieving detachment. It seemed as if I was peeping into another family's life, as if these activities, these signs of unsettling, were not really happening to me. If ever I had felt loneliness, the proverbial loneliness of the only child, it was in those two nightmarish months of January and February as I watched my life unravel – and I could do nothing about it.

In February, for a brief time, I was distracted by the tragedy of Munich and the death of the Manchester United players. Bicycling to school with the others – Alan and Graham (who had also passed his 11-plus in the past year and was now a Bemrose boy) and one or two others who lived near us – we talked about the aircrash in subdued tones. I doubt if we felt sorrow for the deaths as deaths; death was still too abstract a thing for us. But we were awestruck by the idea that these players who were almost household names among football fans had disappeared overnight. Our awe, our sense of incomprehension, was magnified still further when Duncan Edwards died, for he was larger than life in our consciousness. But we did not cry the way we saw adults cry in newspaper pictures and television footages. We were caught up in the drama of it all.

Eventually, I suppose, I confronted the inevitable. I, too, began to sort through my possessions, to decide what mattered and what did not, what to take with me and what to discard. Looking back on that time, I realize that what mattered most, what I desired to do desperately, was to record images of the sights and sounds of my environment permanently in my mind, to have them almost etched in my memory, so that I could invoke them, see them, hear them, feel their very texture, even smell their sundry scents, at will.

To be sure there were the photographs and my books, my

massive collection of football match programmes (including, most precious of all, the programme for the Manchester United–Real Madrid match played at Old Trafford the year before), my volumes of scrapbooks of newspaper cuttings of footballers and cricketers and a sprinkling of my other favourite sportsmen, the diaries I had kept for the past four years. But I wanted to carry within me the substances of my life.

And so I went on long solitary walks, or took the bus, or rode my bicycle to all those parts of Derby I had come to know intimately at one time or another, places that held one association or another for me. In the jargon of psychology, I was intent in creating mental models of my past.

Some mornings I would wake at dawn, from an uneasy sleep, or to the sound of rain lashing against the windows. When that happened, I would simply lie in bed, and stare up at the ceiling, and think of things. There would be suitcases and boxes all over the room; my possessions were half-packed, and I would see evidence of that in the empty bookshelves gaping unpleasantly at me, in the absence of my 78s and LPs and EPs which had been put in a box, in the blank wall across from my bed where my father's beautiful watercolour painting of Stanley Matthews had hung, and which was now wrapped carefully and consigned to one of those boxes.

One such morning, I suddenly remembered a day several years ago, I was seven or so, and we were living in Nottingham, when I had to go into hospital to have my tonsils removed. As I had undressed and climbed into my bed in the children's ward, I had had the oddest sensation, as if every familiar thing in my life was missing. I had that same feeling as I gazed around me; the room was almost shorn of every shred of its warm, familiar, taken-for-granted trappings.

One dark, blustery Saturday afternoon, I put on my mackintosh, went to the back garden and, ignoring the rain, just stood there. Here, my parents and the Amoses had joked, bantered, laughed, enjoying a summer evening after dinner; here I spent precious moments with their daughter, Pauline, and had openly admired her gleaming hair in the autumn sunlight as she bent down to stroke Flash, their Alsatian; here, Mrs Amos and Mrs Howell and my mother had posed as my father took pictures. They wore my mother's saris, put on with her help. They stood, smiling stiffly into the camera, scarcely daring to breathe in case their saris fell off.

Inside the battered shed at the bottom of the garden, there was now an empty space where my bicycle used to be kept. It was gone; we had sold it to a boy who lived somewhere near the Rec. I had glimpsed the boy riding it on Cowly Street, circling round and round, showing it off to friends, the Blackpool tangerine tape still on the handlebars. I had watched him as in a dream; this machine which had been an extension of my self for the past two-and-a-half years now out there, an attachment to a complete stranger. It was like seeing one's arm or leg on someone else's body.

I thought a lot, those days, of past faces. Of the Howells, of Mr Howell's stentorian version of the 'Robin Hood' ballad which had been a 'hit' in my last year in Ashgate, of the Big Brother poster which was still an enigma in my scheme of things.

I thought of David Newman and our holiday together in Llandudno, and wondered how he was and what he was doing. I would have liked to meet David one more time to say goodbye; I could not bear the thought that David would never know that I had gone away for good. One evening I even started out in the direction of his street but then I hesitated and turned back – why, I cannot say.

I went to see my last match at the Baseball Ground alone. This time I did not stand on the terraces. I persuaded my father to give me the money for a seat in the stands behind one of the goals. That day, I suppose, I did not want the usual worm's-eye view but rather the bird's-eye view of the game, for I wanted to drink in, one final time, the whole scene of which the match itself was only a part.

I scarcely watched the game, I was so intent on soaking in the scene, greedily, as if I was seeing it for the first time, as if I would never see it again, as if I wanted to commit it to memory, as indeed I wished to do. I wanted, one last time, to catch the wise-cracks and ripples of laughter that follow, the good-naturedness, the sudden rage on the faces of the mildest-looking men, the obscenities that would be heard loud and clear above the general noise. I wanted to see from above, once more, the proximity of the spectators to the field of action. I wanted to close my eyes at times, just to listen to the sound.

Several days, I went for walks in the neighbourhood, by myself. I would walk up Wheeldon Avenue, past Graham's house, past where Pat and Tony Moore lived, to the end, turn left onto a street called Park Grange, then onto Newton's Walk, past the secondary modern school which Susan Scattergood, my bicycle 'tutor' attended, then turn left onto Cedar Street and down its slope, back onto Kedleston Road, then right towards Markeaton Park. Or I would cross the street from my house, walk down Redshaw Street, onto Watson Street, turn left, then right onto Mackworth Road and into the Rec. Or, I would walk along Kedleston Road towards town, pass Statham Street where Joyce lived, pass White Street where Moni-*da* had his digs, past Highfield Road down to the Five Lamps intersection – and at this junction I would turn left onto Duffield Road and walk towards Darley Park, or walk straight on, cross the Five Lamps Roundabout, past the Convent School, along Bridgegate, past the cathedral, onto Market Square.

A commonplace network of streets, unproblematic, undistinguished, indistinguishable from thousands of other streets in the towns and cities of England. Even I understood that. But utterly unique for me, for it was a web of rich dense associations, what psychologists would call an engram of my evolution from child to teenage boy.

Each street I walked on held a tiny fragment of my life. At the top of Wheeldon Avenue stood a house where a boy from Ashgate lived. For a brief while we were close friends, for we would walk together to school and back. I watched an FA Cup Final in his living room, the one in which Bert Trautmann, the Manchester City goalkeeper, broke a bone in his neck. This boy did not pass the 11-plus, so his parents sent him off to a boarding school after that. When the summer holidays started at the end of my first Bemrose year, Graham and I ran into this boy on Wheeldon Avenue; he almost chose not to recognize us. He had also picked up the poshest accent I had ever heard in Derby – and in less than a year.

On Redshaw Street, the scene of my bicycle lessons, lived another of the boys I knew intensely for a while. He lived with his mother who was, as far as I knew, a widow. He was a quiet boy and an enthusiastic collector of birds' eggs. He was also the most bookish of the boys I knew in the neighbourhood, and my great pleasure was to dip into his library of adventure stories, including a large collection of Biggles books.

At the top of Wheeldon Avenue, if we went past Park Grange, we'd come upon a narrow lane bordered by wooden fence on one side, where we would sometimes lounge about and Tony Moore would perch on the fence, waiting for the girl he was smitten with, to whom he would offer the refrain from 'Singing the Blues'.

On Cedar Street stood a tiny shop where I bought the comics

Eagle and *Dandy* and *Beano* and *Tiger*, where, before Guy Fawkes Day, I would peer through the display window at the fireworks, ponder a while, then venture in with my spare penny or two to buy a cracker or a Catherine Wheel.

Once, in the evening, after I had dried the dishes for my mother, and tired of the incessant packing and chatter of the impending sea voyage, I walked out of the house onto the road. The days were still short and night had already fallen. There had been a light fog in the afternoon, as I had walked home, but now it had become dense. It dispersed the light streaming from street lamps and passing cars, so that the dark night air was bathed in a ghostly ochre hue.

I loved these kinds of evening. In the past, on nights such as this, Robin Darbyshire and I would cycle up Queensway, past Markeaton Park, pedalling furiously so that the dynamo would transmit pedal-power to electricity well enough for the bicycle light to pierce the fog. We would go up the hill to a distant school where we had our weekly Boy Scout troop meetings, where we learned to tie intricate sailors' knots, read tracks and other mysterious signs to help us survive in the wilderness, light fires by rubbing wood against wood as people did in prehistoric times, cook sausages on camp fires, sing uplifting songs and play other silly games which I eventually tired of. There was something in me that resented regimentation of any sort and after a horrible week's camp somewhere in the Derbyshire Dales, in cold and wet and pure discomfort, I told my parents flatly that I was leaving the Scouts. Robin still pedalled up Queensway for his meetings, so far as I knew.

The waste ground where on Guy Fawkes Day massive bonfires were lit; the row of old folks homes on Broadway, which the Queen once visited and we were given the afternoon off to see her; Darley Park, the only park nearby that had a slope on which we could toboggan when it snowed; the river where Graham and I went to row, by virtue of Mr Dean's membership in the rowing club; and, of course, Markeaton Park and its lake – which was so many things to us: a football ground, an ice skating rink, a cricket pitch, a boating lake, a ravine, a campsite, a place to spy on lovers, a place to lounge about – all depending on the season, the weather, the mood, the interest. I had enjoyed all its faces.

To repeat, a network of humdrum streets, parks, roads, houses, waterways, that bore tiny but vital bits and pieces of my English boyhood.

16

End of an English Boyhood

On my final day at Bemrose, I went to school to discover that I was 'famous'. I enjoyed (if that is the word) the fifteen minutes of fame that Andy Warhol was to say we all deserve. Several of the boys had seen the article on us the day before in the *Derby Evening Telegraph*. There was a largish picture of the three of us, and the headline for the feature read 'SURGEON IS RETURNING TO INDIA'. The article spoke of our five-year sojourn in Derby, and mentioned the annual Christmas tradition my father had established of making models of one sort or another for the ear, nose and throat ward at the infirmary to augment the usual decorations. Over the years, he had made models of Everest, the Niagara Falls, the Swiss resort of St Moritz, and an exquisite church complete with churchyard. Newspaper items on his model for the season would appear every Christmas time.

The article said in boldface: 'The son is a pupil at Bemrose School. His reactions to returning to his homeland are somewhat mixed.'

The boys who had seen the feature told the others, and so that morning, before assembly, I was scrutinized with a great deal of curiosity.

During lunch break, the second-formers of Newton House were called to a meeting. I went without that sense of pleasurable anticipation I invariably felt with any event connected with Newton House. This time, I trooped into the classroom listlessly, knowing that whatever was to be said would have no impact on me.

I was caught quite off guard when I realized that the meeting had been summoned in my honour. I heard as if from a very great distance Bob Wilson speak about me, and then Mr Norville, the housemaster, paid some kind of tribute. Mechanically, part-blinded by tears, I accepted a book signed by Bob, Mr Norville and all the other second-formers. It was called *Sporting Days*, written by someone called J. P. W. Mallalieu, but I scarcely noticed the title or the author's name at that moment. It needed much lip-biting and eye-blinking to preserve self-control. I even managed to stammer out a few words of thanks, though I could never recall later what I said.

In the afternoon, I went to say goodbye to Dr Chapman. I had never been inside the headmaster's study, and I now looked curiously around. It was exactly how I imagined a real scholarly headmaster's study – a 'Doctor's' study – should be.

Dr Chapman scarcely knew me, of course, though like Mr Bennett before him, he would have noticed me. He asked me where I was going and how I felt, nodded at my mumbling reply, said something about India, and then I left after shaking hands. In the outer office, the headmaster's secretary gave me a sympathetic smile.

I said one final goodbye to Bob Wilson. I told him I would write to him and he promised he would write back.

The day of our departure was leaden and shiny; a nasty drizzle fell noiselessly all morning. My friends – Graham and Johnny Newton and Alan Potter and Robin Darbyshire, and perhaps Tony and Pat also, though I cannot exactly recall – came tramping up the stairs and into our sitting room. We did not know what to say to one another, for we had never passed through an experience of this sort before. For a few minutes we tried to make conversation, as if this was just another occasion to loaf around together – but then, what could they say to me, who would not be there on Cup Final day, or at the start of the cricket season, or when they went on hikes, or biking?

Finally, we shook hands almost wordlessly, we promised to write, and to our mutual relief, they left, thumping noisily down the stairs, out through the double doors, onto the rain-drenched street. I stood at the bay window gazing down at their navy-blue raincoated backs and watched till they disappeared round the corner. They did not look back.

The evening before, I had done the round of goodbyes to my friends' parents. Mrs Newton hugged me, her eyes brightly wet, her husband shook my hand gruffly; Graham's parents were about as emotional as I had ever seen adults to be in England. Mrs Dean told me that I will come back one day to see them, and I nodded dumbly. Robin Darbyshire's parents, quiet, restrained, gave me sad, grave smiles. Alan's parents, whom I knew least of them all, shook hands.

Quite a few people came to see us off despite the weather, as we boarded the taxi. My mother's friends, Joyce and Frieda, were there; Moni-*da* was, of course, present – he would catch the train to London in a day or two to accompany us to Tilbury; our Bengali and other Indian friends, those who still lived and worked in Derby, were in attendance, looking sombre, faces drawn. For them, my parents' household had constituted an anchor of security in this alien world, their one home away from home, where they were guaranteed Bengali food, Bengali songs, Bengali conversation and a respite from homesickness.

I do not remember who else was there. Everyone in the neighbourhood knew, of course, that the Doctor and his family were departing. Perhaps Susan Scattergood and her older brother Tony, the butcher's children came strolling across the street from their shop. The day before I had popped next door to see the Heldriches. We had drifted far apart over the years, Harold and I, and I scarcely saw him; sometimes I would run across his younger sisters, Avis and Janice. But the old rapport was gone. Still, to leave without seeing the whole family in whose house I had once spent hours watching afternoon television programmes – *The Cisco Kid*, *Hopalong Cassidy*, *Fabian of Scotland Yard*, and umpteen, now forgotten, shows – would have been unthinkable.

Mr and Mrs Amos came out to see us off. They shook hands with my parents, sadly. Bob Amos was there. I cannot recall whether Pauline had turned up. I would like to think she had.

We stayed in London for two days with an aunt and uncle who had recently arrived with their daughters. This uncle, a military officer in the Indian Army, had a posting in the Indian High Commission. On our first evening, they gave a small dinner party to which Moni-*da*'s friends from Imperial College were invited – and the Biswases.

I met Kumkum and Krishna once more. At first I felt self-conscious and gauche, for in less than one year they looked so much more mature and self-assured. We smiled tentatively across the room. The ice eventually broke and we could talk as animatedly and freely as in the summer before. We talked mostly about pop music, the latest 'hits' by Paul Anka and Michael Holliday. I would never see them again.

We left by SS *Chusan* from Tilbury. Below, on the pier, Moni-*da* stood wearing his beige macintosh, hands in pockets, alongside his friends. He looked ever so glum, ever so lonely. Both my parents, emotional people that they were, were crying – whether for Moni-*da*, whether for England, I did not know. I just stood there. I was dry-eyed.

Postscript

In later life I would learn that the word 'revolution' has two meanings. One is the return to an earlier state, as when we speak of the revolution of a wheel or of a planet round the sun. 'What goes round comes around.'

The other meaning refers to a radical break with the past; to bring about a new order.

In my first few months in Calcutta I experienced both kinds of revolution, though in my case they were connected. I, too, had 'revolved' to a prior state: a revolution that took almost a decade to complete. It began in Calcutta and it was in Calcutta that it came to an end on the day the train we had boarded at Victoria Terminus in Bombay – accompanied by my uncle, Mamu, who had been at Bombay to greet us – steamed into Howrah Station three tedious days later.

And just as this first kind of revolution ended, another, of the second kind, began: a complete break with the past, my past, and an entry into a radically new geographic, social and cultural milieu: a new order.

Revolutions of the second kind, I would learn, often have

heavy price tags attached to them. In my case, it swept me up and carried me along like a storm wind and deposited me in a bleak, isolated, solipsistic world. In those first few months in Calcutta, I felt I had been left shipwrecked on an island universe of my own.

Not that there was anything bleak or solipsistic about Calcutta. By my fourteenth birthday, I had already begun to enjoy the peculiar, perverse charms of the city. Compared to Calcutta, Derby seemed a pallid backwater. Very soon, within the year, I made a tiny part of the city my very own, a few square miles that formed a narrow, irregular polygon, whose corners were 26 Amir Ali Avenue, our new home; the junction called Park Circus; the house at 47 Theatre Road that was my mother's parental home – where my maternal grandmother and Mamu and Mimi and their two daughters, and a huge ménage of grandaunts and granduncles and aunts and uncles and cousins lived, where I had been born; La Martiniere for Boys, my new school on Loudon Street; and the British Council Library at the far end of Theatre Road.

So the city per se was not the problem. Yet it invoked odd sensations of a kind I could never convey to anyone.

I would sometimes awake at dawn to a cock crowing somewhere, probably the nearby Karaya Bazaar. I would lie perfectly still on my back, staring up at the whirring ceiling fan and listen to the sound of the neighbourhood rousing itself to the day's business: the first prayer call at the mosque (*masjid*) on a nearby street, the tinkle of the rickshaw-puller's handbells, the raucous cawing of crows, the clank of someone working the handle of the municipal water pump across the road, the yelp of a street mongrel being chased away and, of course, every few minutes, the shrieking, clanging din of electric trams passing by on their tracks on the road just beyond my bedroom windows. What sounds did I hear from my bed in Derby? All I could recall were the occasional birdcalls, the plaintive cheep of sparrows mostly, and the smooth hum of the electric trolley buses.

This contrast was just one manifestation of the sense of unreality that enveloped me from the moment I stepped off the train. Contrasting 'there' from 'here' became a private pastime, almost an obsession.

As for my relatives – the plethora of cousins and aunts and uncles on both my mother's and father's sides – I could find no fault with them. On the contrary. From the instant their smiling, expectant faces floated into view at the train station, I was smothered by their affection, their attention, their fascinated interest. I was like a circus animal or an interesting, intricate toy. They showed me off; they made me speak in English just to savour my Derby accent; they also made gentle fun of my Bengali vocabulary.

Yet, paradoxically, when they asked me about my life in England, it was then I felt most alone, most helpless. Because what they wanted to know was a kind of confirmation of what they already knew about 'life in England' from books and magazines and the intricate public history of relations between Britain and India.

How could I explain my life in England? How could I describe what it was like to bike along miles of leafy country lanes with low walls of jagged, grey stones, sipping orange juice from plastic flasks? And how it was to walk along narrow footpaths that stretched like long ribbons across gently undulating, neatly partitioned fields and ending at stiles on which we would sit and munch sandwiches? And the streams we would pause at? And the little gully we liked to imagine was a ravine, skirting Markeaton Park, which we would cross by walking precariously on tree trunks that served as bridges?

How could I explain the Saturday morning football games we

played against unknown teams in strange places? And the train journeys we would make to Wolverhampton and Sheffield and Leeds and Nottingham to watch our favourite football clubs play? And drives in Graham's dad's car down ramrod-straight roads built in Roman times?

How could I explain that my life over there meant strange place names: the French-sounding Ashby-de-la-Zouche, and Ilkeston and Osmaston and Alfreton that sounded Nordic and Viking to the ear, and Quarndon and Bolsover and Uttoxeter and Littleover which reminded me always of goblins and elfins – and of Noddy and Big Ears.

How could I explain the significance of utterly ordinary things – the football, the cricket, my school, the town itself? Our loafing about Market Square, wandering into the public library, huddling together in soundproof booths at Dixons listening to Elvis and Buddy Holly and the Everly Brothers?

How could I explain the sounds: John Arlott's slow, gentle voice on the radio, commentating on the test match; the signature tune of the radio programme *Music While You Work*; the gossipy, comforting voice of 'Mrs Dale' I would hear on reaching home from school, as my mother listened intently and avidly to *Mrs Dale's Diary*; the news read in 'BBC English'; the Wembley crowd singing 'Abide with Me'; the fruity tones of Kenneth Wolstenholme; the measured, impersonal, anonymous voice announcing the results of the league matches on Saturday evenings?

All that was my life in England. How could I possibly explain it to anyone? It was not for talking about. It was for feeling, for thinking about, as I walked back home from my new school, or in the early morning lying in bed, or while taking a shower.

I would take out my scrapbooks and stare at the pictures of the football teams I had mounted on its pages. I gazed at the glossy

photo of the Derby County team given to us the time Graham
and I visited the *Telegraph* office. I would look at the photograph
of the Newton House first-form football team, with me, the
darkest and slightest, sitting in front, and mouth silently the
names of my teammates. I would open the book presented
to me that last day in Bemrose, *Sporting Days*, and stare at the
signatures.

In my exploratory wanderings about 'my' corner of Calcutta –
which was gradually, tentatively expanding in scope – I would
stumble unexpectedly upon reminders of that life: the sight of
rowers skimming the placid waters of the Dhakuria Lakes; the
velvety smooth sound of Perry Como's voice drifting out of a
ground-floor window near Park Circus as I walked by, singing
'Catch a Falling Star'; a violin rendition of the 'German Lullaby'
on the radio.

Strolling along the narrow aisles inside the New Market, I once
came to an abrupt standstill when I spotted copies of the *Tiger*
weekly. I embraced them as long-lost possessions and bought
several back issues. As I scanned through their pages I was swept
back to dark, dank, winter mornings at the kitchen table, gulping
hateful porridge for breakfast, absorbed in the latest footballing
adventures of Roy Race and the Melchester Rovers Football Club,
or the air battles of Second World War ace pilot Rockfist Rogan.

I established a daily ritual of visiting the British Council
Library after school. In the periodicals room I tried to follow the
fortunes of Blackpool and Derby County from the pages of the
Manchester Guardian. It was the same newspaper my father used
to get, the one I would read. Yet, this lovely building, that immaculately manicured lawn outside, the people sitting beside me –
they all seemed far removed from those football matches, those
scores, those names. Blackpool no longer seemed my Blackpool,
nor Derby County my Derby County. I was out of the culture

and the intimacy of the English football scene. Gradually, my examination of the football results became less enthusiastic, more a force of habit. My eyes would perfunctorily seek out the names of my two teams on the sports pages. I would read new names that made no impression on me. Soon the football came to mean nothing.

I exchanged letters with my friends. Alan, the most lucidly literate amongst them, wrote most often in his well-modulated script giving details of things, gossip about friends. I replied eagerly as soon as his letters arrived. The others wrote, but much less often, less articulate, as if this was an unfamiliar activity for them (as indeed it was). When I sat at my desk to reply, for those minutes I would forget I was in Calcutta. I wrote as if I was somewhere on my annual holiday and would soon be back over there.

Bob Wilson spent an extra year in Bemrose to increase his chances for a scholarship to Oxford. He remained school captain for that year. His letters, written in small but clear script in royal blue ink, were rich in information about Bemrose matters. Once more, it failed to occur to me how remarkable it was for a very busy, very senior boy-turned-man to make time to write to a boy four or five years younger, five thousand miles away, whom he would never meet again. As in the first form, I found it perfectly natural.

Bob won his scholarship to Oxford. He wrote once from there and after relating what life was like, and that he had met a girl from the Continent, he ended by saying that now he was at university and I was, no doubt, occupied with my new life, we would not have much time to write to each other. He hoped I would understand. It was his last letter.

And so, one by one, the correspondences tapered off. The final remnants of my English life were all but gone. Only Moni-*da* prevailed. For two years, the duration of the rest of his tenure in

England, we wrote to each other steadily, regularly. What first-hand news I got about England was from him – though not about Derby, for he had moved away to London for better prospects and to be with his friends.

As for my parents, the rivulet of their lives merged quickly and effortlessly into the main river of their families' lives. They became as one with the others. My father established his private practice in one wing of the large flat we leased on Amir Ali Avenue, put up a shiny new plate with his name and a string of letters after it, and was soon embroiled in his work. If he had had any qualms about returning to India, they must have been dispelled very quickly: within the year he was achieving the professional and financial success that had eventually eluded him in England.

With success came flamboyance. He disdained the new breed of Indian-made cars and purchased instead an American car, a huge 1952 Buick Eight, black and cream in colour, very prominent, unmistakable, unique, as it went about its majestic way on the streets of Calcutta. He acquired a chauffeur, an Anglo-Indian by the name of Thomas.

Thomas was fascinated to learn that we had lived in England for so long – the elusive spiritual home of his community. I struck up a friendship of sorts with him. He plied me with questions about England, and told me of his dream to migrate one day, when he had saved enough money. He would speak of his plans in a wistful tone. I felt rather sorry for him.

With success came Anglicization – the Indian kind: membership at the Calcutta Club; New Year's Eve dinner and dance, for which my father wore, for the first time I could remember, a white shark-skin dinner jacket and a black bow tie, where at last my parents could put into practice the dance steps they had once learned.

With success came sartorial elegance. My father had always dressed well, but now I saw him in a new light, and I had to admit that he cut a very fine figure when, entertaining guests, he would wear a crisp, white, lightly embroidered *kurta* and matching pyjamas with white and gold *nagrai* slippers.

My mother could not recover her place in the hurly-burly of the commercial musical scene. She had been away for too long, she had forgotten its intricate politics. She did not seem to mind. Her old recordings of Tagore songs were still played on the radio, occasionally – and this sufficed. She was content to sing gratis at this concert or that, at private soirées in the intimacy of people's homes. Within weeks of our return, as the monsoon descended upon Calcutta, she gathered her cousins and nephews and nieces and held a *barsha mangal* – a programme of Tagore's songs of the rainy season – in the grand drawing room at 47 Theatre Road. The following spring, she and my aunts held a *basanta utsab* – a festival of dance and *Rabindra-sangeet* celebrating spring – on the majestic lawn of the Theatre Road house, under a balmy clear sky.

For my mother, there was no radical break with the past; no new order. Only the resumption, after a rude, decade-long interruption, of what had always been.

Occasionally, my parents would welcome to the flat a few of the bachelors we had known in Nottingham and Derby, who had returned to Calcutta. No longer bachelors, no longer young, but pot-bellied, married, some balding, some prematurely greying, some successful since returning, some disappointed with the way things had turned out, some came in cars, some in taxis, some on buses or trams, all entombed in family affairs, distracted by the burdens of their life. The one bachelor who remained a bachelor was Mihir-*da*.

And when they came to us, for those few hours they would shed their harassed looks. Roused by shared slivers of English memories, they would laugh and chatter about things past, of Sunday trips to Matlock Bath or Dove Dale, of slow afternoons boating on the lake in Markeaton Park, of loud, argumentative rubbers of bridge on freezing Saturday afternoons huddled close to the coal fire in our living room. They would retell tales about lonely, widowed, over-maternal landladies. And while they talked, their wives, wearing patient, frozen smiles, would look on tolerantly.

As for me, I slowly learned to love the raucous, slogan-filled, dust-encrusted, culture-soaked, politics-obsessed city which was Calcutta. Almost imperceptibly, I discarded my English past; I lost my Derby accent. I strove to be a 'typical' Bengali of the *bhadrolok* class.

My boyhood progressively receded into the deepest recesses of my memory. By the time I was in college and was haunting the coffee houses, so remote did that past seem, I could scarcely believe it was ever real. My boyhood seemed like the memory of a dream. It became a personal mythology.

Yet, such was the power of this mythology, it would intrude on my conscious, everyday existence at the oddest, most unexpected moments. A chance overheard remark, a face glimpsed in the crowd, a laugh, a fragrance of some perfume wafting by, a tune, a breeze blowing in a particular way, an item in a newspaper, an essay read over coffee would suddenly set off a chain of associations, spawn a collage of images and emotions and sounds that would engulf and overwhelm me. And then I would feel shattered.

One evening I finally saw the BBC film of the 1953 FA Cup Final, the *Matthews Cup Final*. I saw it in the most unlikely place I could imagine, in the auditorium on the campus of Bengal Engineering College in Sibpur, where I was then an undergraduate. There, a few hundred yards from the River Ganga, in a crowd of mostly Bengali students, I saw unfold before my eyes, the plays, the passes, the dribbles, the shots, the goals, the saves I had once known by heart.

There they all were! Stanley Matthews with his elderly stoop; the good-looking Stanley Mortensen; the lanky, balding captain Harry Johnston; the well-combed George Farm in goal; the tiny inside forwards Ernie Taylor and Jackie Mudie; the swarthy Bill Perry. It was while watching the game amid a throng of three or four hundred that I felt an emotion I had forgotten. It was a sense of immense aloneness, apartness, alienation – the kind I had experienced those first few weeks after returning to Calcutta five years earlier. The fact was, we were watching two different games – my fellow students and I. They were seeing an exciting football match. I was witnessing a newsreel of a fragment of my life. I was reliving a whole network of experiences. I think it was then that I realized this: I could never be a 'typical' Bengali or a 'typical' Indian. I was instead, quite unwittingly, the kind of person Thomas Macaulay in the nineteenth century had talked of when he wrote of persons 'Indian in blood or colour but English in taste'. My English boyhood had forever situated me in this Macaulayesque state of existence.

At last, as the game came to a frantic climax, I saw the magic: Blackpool magic, black magic, Matthews magic. Ernie Taylor plying Matthews with clever, sly passes, Matthews darting up the right wing, doing all the things I knew he had done, loping towards a defender, standing momentarily perfectly still, showing the ball to the opponent, daring him, swaying slightly to the inside, the defender following his motion, hesitantly, warily lunging in that direction, and then Matthews had gone around him, on the outside, hugging the touchline, and then past another defender, then that unbelievable, sudden spurt within a space of just a few yards, leaving the opponent dawdling, embarrassed, and there was Matthews near the corner flag, and then a centre, once, twice, and again, and the commentator, Kenneth Wolstenholme's voice rising to reach above the noise of the Wembley crowd, and just as it seemed almost certain that the referee must blow his whistle and extra time would ensue, there was Matthews again, leaving hapless defenders sprawling absurdly on the grass, and then he centred once more just before slipping himself, and the camera desperately swivelling to follow the ball, and almost missing Bill Perry, the outside left, banging the ball into the goal, and there was Mortensen's arms outstretched in triumph, and Perry's arms outstretched, and there was Matthews, rushing towards Perry. Then it was all over.